DREAM-WALKING

DREAM-WALKING

THE SACRED

DIMENSION OF

DISCIPLESHIP

LARRY L. NIEMEYER

WinePressPublishing
Great Books, Defined.

WinePress Publishing (PO Box 428, Enumclaw, WA 98022) functions only as book publisher. As such, the ultimate design, content, editorial accuracy, and views expressed or implied in this work are those of the author.

This book offers readers thirty-three ways to interact with the contents, and it is suggested that they either purchase A Dream-walking Journal from www.harvest21.org or download a copy from the same website and create their own computerized Dream-walking Journal.

ISBN 13: 978-1-4141-1914-4
ISBN 10: 1-4141-1914-3
Library of Congress Catalog Card Number: 2010912447

CONTENTS

PREFACE

JESUS WAS A dream-walker—*the* dream-walker. However we have not understood the dream, and we have misconstrued the walk. I have declared and described the dream in my previous book[1] where I applied it to Adam and Eve as well as to all their descendants since the beginning. That dream is God's desire to bring his LIFE[2] to the life of every human being who will accept it. Before the beginning of time, he determined that human life—fearfully and wonderfully made—would be miraculously redeemed and completed by his own design. His dream is the gospel itself.

As to the walk, we have long admired Christ's thirty-year walk on earth. He exemplified truth, integrity, authority, love, courage, and an uncompromising spirit. He healed the sick, the blind, lame, and leprous. He miraculously fed thousands, contributed to social occasions, enriched fishermen, and even calmed storms. He walked on water, raised Lazarus, and rose from the grave.

So how does that walk link to the dream? First, Christ was the very embodiment of God's dream, perfect divine LIFE in a normal human life. He was the LIFE-in-life man par excellence. He blended divine LIFE and human life perfectly. He was the very incarnation of God's dream. He walked the dream.

Second, as Son of God, he ensured that everyone who would listen knew that the Father's dream was the reason for his every word, deed, response, reaction, act of love, illustration, demonstration, and relationship. He made this very plain:

> I tell you the truth, the Son can do nothing by himself; he can do only what he sees his Father doing, because whatever the Father does the Son also does.
>
> —John 5:19

> By myself I can do nothing; I judge only as I hear, and my judgment is just, for I seek not to please myself but him who sent me.
>
> —John 5:30

> For the very work that the Father has given me to finish, and which I am doing, testifies that the Father has sent me.
>
> —John 5:36

When Christ obeyed the Father's will he sustained the Father's dream; LIFE would dwell in human life made holy. That dream was formulated in eternity, and his task was to track faithfully and patiently fulfill that dream in time. He walked the dream.

Third, Jesus came to make LIFE available to all of us and to turn us into dream-walkers. He died to remove all sin that is abhorred by LIFE. He rose from the grave to prove that LIFE is the end sought by God, not death. He died and rose again to turn us into LIFE-in-life people borne along on the Father's sacred dream.

I challenge you to grasp this dream as never before and walk it with Jesus.

INTRODUCTION

THE APOSTLE JOHN walked with Jesus for three years during the Lord's ministry. He walked with the dream-walker, but he never grasped the significance of the dream until the Resurrection. After the Resurrection, John finally began understanding Christ's LIFE-in-life existence. Even then, he dawdled for fifty fateful days—crawling, stumbling, and falling. Finally, at the end of Christ's forty days of post-resurrection appearances, John and others experienced the coming of LIFE to their own lives. Ten days later came Pentecost, when the Holy Spirit descended with power on the apostles. From those days on, John no longer simply walked. Rather, he became a dream-walker. His life was no longer just a walk with Jesus; it was a walk like that of Jesus. The LIFE of the Father who had energized Jesus became the LIFE that energized John. He finally accepted what it took to be a dream-walker: God's LIFE within.

In this book, John's story will remind us of our own. We will follow his life through some of his activities, including his discipleship mobilization of others. Because the apostle's story reminds me of my own story, I will tell some of that. My hope is that by the time we look at Jesus more intimately, and John more objectively, we should be ready to look at ourselves more honestly.

Many Christians sleepwalk through their Christian lives when they ought to be dream-walking. They stumble, walking in a daze. Many do not even consider, let alone understand, God's dream. The malady is not new. In his letter to the Romans, the apostle Paul said, "And do this, understanding the present time. The hour has come for you to wake up from your slumber, because our salvation is nearer now than when we first believed" (13:11).

Begin your dream-walking journal right away. Here is the first reflective exercise to which you may respond in the version of the journal you have chosen. Share the results with someone else, perhaps a new disciple, who may need to walk with the Lord in new ways.

---

1. "Sleep-walking" may seem a bit unkind, an inconsiderate assessment of your present condition. What do you think? Are there some conditions in your life that might fit the description? Explain.

This book is a follow up to *God's Dream*. That book highlighted God's desire to bring his LIFE to every human life acknowledging eternal hope in Jesus Christ. It offered a refreshing look at the gospel. In this book, *Dream-Walking*, I offer a sacred view of discipleship—or what it means to follow Jesus. Both books begin at the wonder of God's dream as it is declared, for example, in Ephesians 1:3-6:

> Praise be to the God and Father of our Lord Jesus Christ, who has blessed us in the heavenly realms with every spiritual blessing in Christ. For he chose us in him before the creation of the world to be holy and blameless in his sight. In love he predestined us to be adopted as his sons through Jesus Christ, in accordance with his pleasure and will—to the praise of his glorious grace, which he has freely given us in the One he loves.

Discipleship, as intended by God, rises straight out of being chosen in Christ to share the Father's gospel dream. No earthly doctrine claiming good news comes close to the eternal dream of God's Good News to bring his LIFE to every human life that will receive him. In the same way, no religious activities come close to the place of discipleship in God's dream.

I hope to help you walk in God's dream by the sacred dimensions of discipleship. I want to help you walk that dream with a spring in your step, a glow in your eyes, and passion in your heart. My thoughts are drawn to Peter and John's results when they shared God's LIFE with a wounded life.

> Then Peter said, "Silver and gold I do not have, but what I have I give you. In the name of Jesus Christ of Nazareth, walk." Taking him by the right hand, he helped him up, and instantly the man's feet and ankles became strong. He jumped to his feet and began to walk. Then he went with them into the temple courts, walking and jumping, and praising God.
>
> —Acts 3:6-8

The apostles lacked financial resources, but they gave the best thing they had: the wonderful gift of God's LIFE. They had become vessels of that LIFE. The man in the third chapter of Acts had been crippled from birth. He did not see his wealth increase after meeting Peter, but he did stand up and walk. Perhaps, like that once-wounded man, some of you will go on to dance, jump, and leap. That is my hope. If there is a desire in your life to walk like Jesus as never before, I hope God uses this book to give you that noble desire.

---

2. What previous experience(s), if any, have you had in discipleship? Describe it/them briefly. In what way could "dream-walking" take you to new dimensions?

PART 1

PERSONAL JOURNEYS TO THE DREAM-WALK

Our lives must somehow encounter God's dream. Though we may have heard the gospel in this way or that, we must finally come to the realization that the divine nature of the gospel lays claim to both our personal and corporate worlds.

In this first part of the book, I present my personal journey as an encouragement for you to identify your own path. By *path* I do not mean religion, church, denomination, institution, or association. Instead, I refer to a path to God's dream. That is why I wrote *God's Dream*, to help readers consider where they have been and where they could be.

After considering my path and encouraging you to write about yours, this first part takes a look at how one man became a *dream-walker*. The term may be new, but the path is as old as the Bible. By tracing aspects of the apostle John's journey toward God's gospel dream as a disciple, we can see the wonderful potential of God's LIFE in a human life. It was when John finally realized the divine nature of the gospel that he was able to reflect on his three years with Christ and truly prepare for what would be a fifty-to-sixty year ministry bringing God's LIFE to the center of people's lives.

CHAPTER 1

. . . .

A PERSONAL ENCOUNTER
WITH GOD'S GOSPEL DREAM

DISCIPLESHIP BEGAN AS a dream in my life—my own dream.

After a thirteen-year church planting mission to the African countries of Zimbabwe and Zambia from 1966 to 1979, God finally got my attention with the Great Commission in Matthew 28:19-20: "Go and make disciples of all nations, baptizing them in the name of the Father and of the Son and of the Holy Spirit, and teaching them to obey everything I have commanded you. And surely I am with you always, to the very end of the age." I was certainly not ignorant of the Great Commission, but I had allowed it to refer to any and all of my missionary activities. I had been too busy being a missionary and learning cultures and languages, building, traveling, spreading the gospel, starting churches, training, and writing—all this with my wife and first son.

My story is about a costly beginning and an eventual discipleship mobilization.

A COSTLY BEGINNING

Knowledge of God's dream will change a person, and those changes will bring a life-changing personal story. It was so with me. While everyone's story is unique, let me tell you how I finally

1

came to encounter God's dream—and got beyond my own dream. As I tell my story, you may want to think about your own.

The Death of a Friend

Through the death of a friend in the 1970s God began the way of changing my understanding of the gospel and its application to every aspect of life, including discipleship mobilization. I met Tom at an Arizona youth camp in 1972 where my wife and I were the missionary speakers and he was the worship leader. We told stories of faith; Tom sang his story accompanied by his guitar. His worship leadership style was always punctuated by a phrase that became very familiar to us: "Praise God."

"Let's worship and sing some songs. Praise God."

"That was good. Praise God."

He would strum a few chords and say, "Praise God."

Our follow-up mission message wasn't half as exhilarating as Tom's music ministry, and I envied his rapport with the youth and his ability to so easily focus on God. Beneath my breath, I began murmuring, *What will "praise God Tom" have for us today?* That was a bad attitude.

The camp ended and soon we moved to Zambia, while Tom returned to his Arizona youth ministry. We started getting letters from Tom filled with news and other matters. Funny thing, they were also punctuated the same way: "Praise God." At the top of the letter, down at the bottom, scattered throughout the message, scribbled in the margins was the phrase "Praise God." There was more. Tom often included a cassette or two of music. Some of the songs were by different artists and he also sang some to his own guitar accompaniment. Same punctuation: "Praise God." I started feeling bad about my attitude at the youth camp.

Months passed, and the letters continued. Tom resigned his youth ministry position and joined the U. S. Army. "Praise God." He met the love of his life and they married. "Praise God." "Come on honey, say hi to Larry and Judy. Praise God." Later, they were expecting a baby. "Praise God." We so enjoyed Tom's ministry from a distance.

One day we realized we had not received a letter for quite a while. Tom was busy with new responsibilities, a new wife, and a baby coming. Finally, a letter came, but not from Tom. His wife wrote to say there would be no more letters from Tom. They had decided to take a vacation at the coast before the baby came. During those days together, Tom went swimming and died in a powerful Atlantic undertow.

The news saddened us deeply and convicted me again of my original attitude toward Tom. In bed that hot, humid night in Zambia, I reflected on Tom's loving ministry to us. We had been so fortunate. Then I tried to relive his last moments of life in the ocean—swimming, then caught by the watery pressure of that undertow, surprised by its power and intensity. Fighting to get to the surface but continually dragged to murky depths. Fighting for air but gulping water. Fighting for light but weakened in darkness. Strength spent. A cold brine.

Then a new insight filled my heart. The final thoughts rushing through Tom's struggling mind must have included the words that punctuated his life as I knew it: "Praise God." And he drowned.

Then, in his mysterious way, God prompted a question in my mind that night. *Larry, if you died tonight, would people know that your life was as focused on me as was Tom's?* I had to admit that if I died that night, people would vaguely remember me as a good man, a hard worker, a church person, always active, a determined servant of God. But they would not think of me as one who honored God's centrality in my life. He was there—somehow. But he was not the central focus. No.

That night, God began a long process of change in my life. He prompted me the next day to start living with him at the center of my being and to start helping others come to that clear, concise, covenant centrality. That was when discipleship became all-important to my ministry. Unfortunately, I didn't go very deep into God's will during those days, and discipleship soon became my dream rather than his.

The Birth of Discipleship

I could describe at length my feeble attempts in those beginning years. The task was hard. I had never been discipled in my Christian life. I was just taught, told, taught, told, and taught again. Because I was never discipled, I didn't know how to disciple others. I had no clue how to begin. Books on discipleship were few in the 1970s, at least in Zambia. I tried, however, right there. I spoke the Bemba language with my first group of disciples, some of whom could not read or write. By 1979 I knew my emphasis on discipleship would require new resources, companions, and skills. God was faithful and graciously brought those necessities together in a three-year furlough in the USA.

During the furlough I developed a nine-month weekly tool for people to respond to sixty possible God-centered transformations. The proposed relationships began with a sharing of biblical confidence, consistency, and stability—the foundations for discipleship mobilization. I call this the foundation series. It led into a time of sharing Christlikeness, evangelism, and discipling, which offer the fruitfulness of discipleship mobilization. I call this the fruitfulness series.[3]

Those original tools were given a chance in my own home church in America's Northwest, and we began seeing fruit. I will always be grateful to Don Cox, the church, and the leadership for allowing me to give the materials a dry run.

By 1982, Judy and I were ready to return to Africa with our two adopted sons. This time our destination was Kenya. Conscious of the new context, we did not rush into discipleship implementation. African friends finally persuaded us to use what we had developed, and so we slowly began preparing it for the new setting. After seven years, we had developed only ninety people as disciples. Mission colleagues had come and gone with little enthusiasm for the possibilities.

Why the slow growth? I began seeing how the human dimensions of discipleship often negate the sacred possibilities of maturity, mobilization, and multiplication. Human-centered timeframes, commitments, and loyalties often undid the sacred possibilities. The

4

human dimensions interfered rather than inspired, tore down rather than built up, hindered rather than helped. Out of ten new disciples who began the journey, eight finished the foundation series, five finished the fruitfulness series, and only two or three went on to make disciples of their own. Mobilization and multiplication were stymied.

Our idealistic goal of doubling every year eventually became a goal of doubling every two years—and then every four to five years. Those who dropped out of the relationship early did so because of those human dimensions: There were too many other activities; there was no time left in the busy day; and there were too many other options, competing relationships, and other resources.

Some were intimidated by the commitment that was expected to experience transformation. Some just chose not to obey the Lord in the basics. Some believers were even discouraged by their own Christian friends and church leaders who did not support their engagement in discipleship training and evangelization. Those who dropped out beyond the first series did so because they gradually lost any interest in going on to share Christlikeness, evangelism, and discipling as a continually expanding outreach under Christ's control.

At the same time I began seeing how the secular world distracts many from discipleship mobilization. During this twenty-six-year effort since 1984, I wrote a book on how fourteen features of modernity negate discipleship efforts.[4] It was an unsettling exercise, salvaged only by a parallel study of Luke's gospel showing Jesus confronting each of those issues. Our efforts to seek God-centered results were being implemented in an age submerged in words, an age overrun with knowledge.[5] As Os Guinness has said, it was an age with "a flood of knowledge but only a drop of wisdom."[6] We were working at a time when many were blindly cutting themselves loose from God, his plan, and his dream.

I became increasingly gripped by the way discipleship activity fit within God's kingdom plan.[7] While trying to maintain the momentum, I began mixing greater quantities of God's plan into my teaching and training. Those efforts finally led to my realizing that discipleship is God's dream, not mine. It is a dream within his larger eternal kingdom plan.

On to Discipleship Mobilization

By God's grace, the results of those twenty-six years on the field were significant. We mobilized 26,000 disciples, saw 7,000 of them become disciple-makers, and equipped 1,300 men and women to become discipleship team leaders in a variety of churches and communities. The movement continues to this day, though we deliberately remained small as an institution; we were intent on not building a mission, but rather a movement.

Reflecting on that early work, I now realize that the discipleship books I used were very much the paint-by-number or fill-in-the-blank approach that was popular thirty to forty years ago. That approach was helpful to some people, especially those of more phlegmatic and melancholic personalities. They have a steady, loyal, and conscientious disposition. Such people become satisfied with a practical approach that is worthy, continuous, and solid.

Yet others wanted and needed more and those early tools did not provide the boost they sought. They wanted venture, surprise, newness, and life on tiptoe. Those people were the action-oriented and sociable types—the choleric and sanguine. Some wanted to paint with a flourish—none of that paint-by-number stuff. Some wanted to write their own stories rather than fill in the blanks of workbook-style publications. Increasingly I wanted to give them such tools.

My concern in this book, then, is first to reinforce and encourage those who faithfully implement those original tools. Second, I want to present a way to reach the seven or eight out of every ten Christians who drop out of a methodical approach to discipleship. I want to appeal to those seeking:

- experience more than explanation
- direction more than devices
- action more than activity, and
- results more than routines.

I want this book to support my previous foundations and fruitfulness for discipleship mobilization, but I also want it to take us beyond those approaches.

My goal is to add 100,000 new disciples to the current 26,000 developed in my first twenty-six years of work. I want to add those new disciples by the year 2016 and give them effective tools for the task of mobilizing even more disciples of Christ. As the apostle Paul put it, "And the things you have heard me say in the presence of many witnesses entrust to reliable men who will also be qualified to teach others" (2 Tim. 2:2). I hope this book contributes to that goal.

· ·

CHAPTER 2

BECOMING
A DREAM-WALKER

SOME CHRISTIANS ARE only scooting or crawling along in their Christian lives because they have not gained the confidence, consistency, and stability of dream-walking. We have all eagerly watched babies begin rolling over from belly to back, with arms and legs flailing, raising themselves and scooting along on their stomachs, and finally beginning to crawl—so cute. Such proud moments. However, we would be direly concerned if those babies never got beyond that stage.

The same could be said if they took but one step—and stopped. A baby's first step brings delight. Upright, they wave their arms for balance while their feet remain firmly planted as if each weighed a ton. First steps are often more like first stomps—picking up one foot excessively high and dropping it like a sumo wrestler preparing to fight. Sometimes parents hand the babies off to each other and friends, everyone coaxing them to take another step.

I remember those days with our two sons. (We had waited eight years for the adoption of our first son, and seven more for the second.) With their hands holding on to my index fingers, we would chase along after a soccer ball even before they could walk on their own. Soon they were walking on their own, and yes, they continued chasing a soccer ball for at least the next twenty-six years. My wife and I became eager spectators.

WALKING, NOT SCOOTING

God is just as eager for us to get beyond the scooting and crawling stages of our Christian development. Maybe the picture of a baby walking in front of a parent while holding to index fingers can illustrate two Scriptures in the Psalms:

> For you have delivered me from death and my feet from stumbling, that I may walk before God in the light of life.
>
> —Ps. 56:13

> For you, O Lord, have delivered my soul from death, my eyes from tears, my feet from stumbling, that I may walk before the Lord in the land of the living.
>
> —Ps. 116:8-9

Notice that we are to walk *before* the Lord, not *behind* him. God is holding us up. Notice also the psalmist's reference in both Scriptures to life—"in the light of life" and "in the land of the living." I wonder if that reference could be to LIFE, to God dwelling in us. I can't help thinking so.

There are no Scriptures that encourage us to scoot or crawl. But many tell us to walk. The book of Proverbs contains a host of such verses:

> Leave your simple ways and you will live; walk in the way of understanding.
>
> —Prov. 9:6

> The man of integrity walks securely, but he who takes crooked paths will be found out.
>
> —Prov. 10:9

> He who walks with the wise grows wise, but a companion of fools suffers harm.
>
> —Prov. 13:20

He whose walk is blameless is kept safe, but he whose ways are perverse will suddenly fall.

—Prov. 28:18

The biblical way is to walk, not crawl. And that is a good way to consider discipleship, especially discipleship with sacred dimensions.

WALKING WITH JESUS

As Jesus began his three-year ministry, he looked for disciples and forever set the standard for discipleship. As he found the twelve, he called them to follow him:

As Jesus went on from there, he saw a man named Matthew sitting at the tax collector's booth "Follow me," he told him, and Matthew got up and followed him.

—Matt. 9:9

"Come, follow me," Jesus said, "and I will make you fishers of men."

—Matt. 4:19

Jesus answered, "If you want to be perfect, go, sell your possessions and give to the poor, and you will have treasure in heaven. Then come, follow me."

—Matt. 19:21

Immediately upon giving the invitations, he turned and walked. There was no conference, seminar, or sacred event to attend. There was no well-planned outing, no mountain-climbing challenge, and no purchase to make. The Bible says he just turned around and walked. And when Jesus walked, the disciples followed. They followed him to the nearby villages, towns, and cities. They followed through markets, pastures and fields, on dusty paths, hilly passages, wind-blown grasslands, hot sand, and crumbling rock. They followed with minimum personal effects, carrying only staffs, some water, and a little food. They followed the Master from sunrise to sunset, and sometimes even in darkness. Their journey took them through springtime freshness, seasonal heat, and brisk cold air. Whatever the circumstance, the disciples followed.

Despite the lengths the disciples went to follow Jesus, they still did not yet walk as he walked. They walked as they always walked and did not know that they walked with LIFE—God's LIFE in Jesus Christ. They walked with "the beginning and the firstborn from among the dead," having no clue as to their own destiny of one day being born again into the same divine family (Col. 1:15-18). Unsuspectingly, they walked with the One who wanted more than anything else to give them his very LIFE: "I have come that they may have LIFE and have it to the full" (John 10:10b, emphasis added). Blindly, they walked with the One who would die to ensure they could receive this gift out of eternity from the Father of LIFE.

It took the disciples a while to grasp such infinite truth. A long while. The Lord's words failed to sink in. They viewed him in typical religious ways, but they had no concept yet of the faith to which he called them, the faith he had defined before the beginning of time:

> Paul, a servant of God and an apostle of Jesus Christ for the faith of God's elect and the knowledge of the truth that leads to godliness—a faith and knowledge resting on the hope of eternal life, which God, who does not lie, promised before the beginning of time, and at his appointed season he brought his word to light through the preaching entrusted to me by the command of God our Savior.
>
> —Titus 1:1-3

The disciples only carelessly observed the Lord's miracles. Their religious expectations had no place for the supernatural. Their final journey to Jerusalem with Jesus left them exhausted and traumatically tired. The gospel of Matthew describes Jesus and the disciples in Gethsemane where he had gone away to pray while the disciples rested: "When he came back, he again found them sleeping, because their eyes were heavy. So he left them and went away once more and prayed the third time, saying the same thing. Then he returned to the disciples and said to them, "Are you still sleeping and resting? Look, the hour is near, and the Son of Man is betrayed into the hands of sinners (26:43-45)."

We are so much like those early disciples, hard to move out of our former ways of thinking. We are bound up with religious notions and have little if any grasp of the uniqueness of our faith. We carelessly observe Christ's life with its teachings, miracles, and incredible actions. We too easily get tired, bored, and indifferent to any challenges for the ultimate journey with Christ.

Perhaps we can relate to the way one of those twelve disciples became a dream-walker.

BECOMING A DREAM-WALKER

The apostle John, who would later write the gospel, his epistles, and the book of Revelation, provides an example. He walked with Jesus from the beginning—and missed so much.

John's Three Years with Jesus

The son of Zebedee and Salome, John was a fisherman on the Sea of Galilee. He had a business partnership with his father, his brother James, and also Peter, succeeding well enough to be able to hire workers (Mark 1:19-20). He and James followed Jesus on the first invitation (Mark 1:20 says that "without delay he called them, and they ... followed him"), but they were not the only ones from the family who followed Christ. Though little else is known about the father, John's mother was also a disciple of the Lord. She served Jesus and was present at both his crucifixion and his resurrection (Matt. 27:56; Mark 16:1).

Jesus designated John, together with his brother James, as a Son of Thunder. John was explosive and spontaneous, intolerant, and narrow-minded. He once tried to turn Jesus away from being compassionate about a man possessed by demons (Mark 9:38). Condemning and judgmental, he wanted to draw lines and make distinctions. Quick-tempered and violent, he was prepared to destroy a Samaritan village because it did not welcome the Lord (Luke 9:54). Scheming and self-centered, he sought a special position in the plans of Jesus (Mark 10:35; Matt. 20:20). His impulsiveness was clear when he declared his readiness to go anywhere with the Lord (Mark 10:39).

In spite of his brazen ways, this apostle, together with James and Peter, became part of Christ's inner circle. As such, he was a personal witness to the raising of Jairus' daughter (Mark 5:37), the transfiguration (Mark 9:2), and the Gethsemane experience (Mark 14:33). John became "the disciple whom Jesus loved," a reference he used to describe himself five times in his own gospel (John 13:23; 19:26; 20:2; 21:7, 20). This special bond was confirmed at the cross, where he was seemingly the only disciple present and when Jesus placed Mary in his care (John 19:25-26). His intimacy with Christ was evident to the other disciples because they expected him to ask Jesus the hard questions about betrayal (John 13:22-25), and they even sought the Lord to clarify John's status (John 21:20).

Yet, despite his position within the Lord's inner circle, John was only scooting and crawling during his three years with Jesus because he was not yet walking as Jesus walked.

> **3.** Reflect on your past three years with Jesus. How would you describe them? Any crawling and scooting? Write a few notes in your journal.

John's Awakening

John's writings in the New Testament testify to a man radically changed. When did that transformation take place? We often think the change came at Pentecost when "Suddenly a sound like the blowing of a violent wind came from heaven" (Acts 2:2). But there was a previous event for John, a turning point for this Son of Thunder. It came at the tomb of Jesus, an event carefully reported by John himself (John 20:1-14). Describing those events, he reports the way he and others responded. One commentator has observed that the word *see* and its variations occur repeatedly in the passage, in John 20:1, 5, 6, 8, 12, and 14, but the Greek word is not the same in each case.[8] Three distinct words are used, each with a different shade of meaning.

In John 20:1, Mary *sees* in the physical sense that the stone has been removed. She reports this to Peter and John, and the two disciples race to the burial site. John, who outran Peter to Jesus' tomb, first *saw* the linen wrappings that same way as he looked in at the tomb's entrance (20:5). The word used for the way both Mary and John saw has the same derivation. Impulsively, Peter ran straight into the tomb and *saw* things in another way as reflected by the Greek word used (20:6). The scene captivated his eyes, just like Mary's were awestruck when she later saw the two angels and Jesus (20:12, 14). In these cases, the word *see* refers first to facts and second to impressions.

A third Greek word is used of John's *seeing* in John 20:8, where we read, "He saw and believed." It describes a special experience and denotes spiritual insight, illumination, perception, knowledge and understanding. John saw, everything became clear, and he believed. Here was John's awakening to the eternal dream of God for his life and every life.

What was the nature of this awakening that led to John's dramatic change? Try to put yourself in his shoes. Perhaps the apostle began to reflect on his three years with Jesus. Had he taken Christ's intentions too lightly? What had he missed? Why had he overlooked the sacred meanings of the Lord's words? Why did he hear it all but understand so little? How could he have seen and yet not have comprehended?

John's witness to the resurrection of Christ was the point in his life when he saw as he had never seen before. "He saw and believed." For the first time, he was struck by the meaning and significance of the LIFE-in-life nature of Jesus Christ. Suddenly he saw the divine LIFE aspect of our Lord. He began to understand what Jesus meant when he said, "For as the Father has LIFE in himself, so he has granted the Son to have LIFE in himself" (John 5:26, emphasis added). A window opened and light streamed in. A barrier was removed.

> **4.** If there has ever been a time in your life when you have been awe-struck by the sacredness and divine nature of Christ, describe that moment. What were the circumstances? What words describe the event? Write some notes when ready.

John's Reflection

In seeing the Resurrection, John saw Jesus as never before. He began seeing what the Lord meant when he said, "I am the resurrection and the LIFE" (John 11:25 emphasis added) and "I am the way the truth and the LIFE" (John 14:6).

Now John began wondering about the place of that LIFE in his own life. For the first time he began stepping out of the shadows of his previous thinking and experience— and into gospel possibilities of life transformation. This was his awakening. John began turning from his own life, acquired at his first birth, to the possibilities of God's LIFE, acquired through Jesus at a second birth. John was seeing the possibilities of being born again, as Jesus had explained to Nicodemus when he said, "I tell you the truth, no one can see the kingdom of God unless he is born again" (John 3:3). That second birth was not just a religious lesson for Nicodemus, but a reality beyond all religious experience. John was no longer preoccupied with his own life, but became transfixed by God's.

At the scene of Christ's resurrection, LIFE became the deciding reality for this apostle. I believe that is why the word is so prominent in his gospel account. That gospel begins and ends with *life*, a word that occurs thirty-five times in the book. We just have to determine when it is a reference to human life and when it refers to divine LIFE. For John, understanding God's LIFE began to redefine everything he knew about his own life. He discovered what others have learned in their own ways:

"It takes God to be a man."

—W. Ian Thomas[9]

"We were meant to be inhabited by God and to live by a power beyond ourselves."

—Dallas Willard[10]

"We don't have it within ourselves to be ourselves."

—Eugene Peterson[11]

"For a human to be truly alive—by our Creator's definition—is to live as an extension of God's own life."

—David C. Needham[12]

John summarized his discovery at the Resurrection in words like those of 1 John 5:12:"He who has the Son has LIFE; he who does not have the Son of God does not have LIFE" (emphasis added). John's awakening gradually turned him from self-centered existence to God-centered exaltation.

The changes in John's life were contrary to all expectations in his Jewish community. Jewish citizens sought conformity in their lives by observing the 613 laws of the Torah and the 3,000 added by the religious leaders. They certainly did not seek change. John's life-changing transformation broke with the expectations of that religious continuity in a daring discontinuity of newfound faith.

Greek citizens sought personal growth and development in their lives. They wanted to gain influence and knowledge. But John did not jump from the Hebrew tradition to the Greek. His transformation was not just a change of knowledge or a greater effort at improvement. John did not ascend to some new religious height. Rather, he descended from pride to humility through genuine repentance. John turned from being the center of life to occupy the sacred position God designed for him.

John surrendered to the truth that alone could change him, the truth that his life needed the LIFE of God within. In yielding to this truth, John placed himself at the beginning of a dream-walking experience. In removing himself from the center of life, he made that center available to LIFE. In doing so, John's life was not destroyed but made perfect, complete.

John's own inspired words in John 1:4 declared the transformation: "In him was LIFE, and that LIFE was the light of men" (emphasis added). E. Stanley Jones expanded on that declaration, and we can apply it to John: "Anything that is in itself is existence; anything that is in God is life."[13] John's body was physical existence, but it would perish like all physical things, but his life in God became LIFE-in-life living.

John had become alive in new ways, opening new opportunities and creating new hope. His life-only existence was non-creative and ineffectual. His LIFE-centered living, however, had become creative and effectual. Even his words in themselves were mere words,—but in Christ they contained LIFE-in-life possibilities. They were living and life-giving, winging their way to the needs of others. His very face in itself was mere existence—uninspiring and un-illuminated; but in God it was a LIFE-in-life face, glowing with glory and shining with the Spirit.

John's reflection upon his awakening resulted in realizing that his life could become everything it had been created to be when finally connected with the LIFE of God. This LIFE was not distant and removed, for John had mingled with him for three years, shared his food, slept, worked, traveled, and worshiped with him. What a LIFE! Yet, so available. What an awakening!

A New Walk with Jesus

At the Resurrection, John had become prepared for a new walk with Jesus. While the Lord had been walking the Father's dream, John had just been walking—perhaps in his own dreams. It was time for a new walk, time for God's dream in John's life.

What were the three elements of John's preparation to dream-walk with Jesus?

- He *walked* with Jesus, though it may have been more like a scoot or a crawl.
- He *followed* the Redeemer for three years.
- He was *awakened* to the reality of LIFE at Christ's resurrection.

These three elements can be applied to our own walk—and our current preparation to walk in new ways. Where are you in your walk with Jesus?

5. In what ways have you realized the presence of God's LIFE in your life?

PART 2

LIFE-FORTIFIED FOUNDATIONS FOR THE WALK

A weak foundation will always result in a weak edifice. In construction, it may be a house, office, or factory. In an organization, it may be a program, product, or service. If the foundation is weak, the outcome will be weak. The same is true of discipleship mobilization. If the foundations are weak, the results will be weak. Foundations for discipleship differ, however. They are organic, having to do with life, not structures or organizations.

The good news for discipleship is that its foundation is not of our making. It does not depend on our connections, networks, skills, resources, charisma, leadership, and commitment. All these help, yet they may be limited for us, even unavailable. But we are given something special for discipleship effectiveness and that is the gift of God's LIFE, available by grace to all. That gift provides the sacred dimension discussed in this book.

In this section, we will continue recognizing the difference God's LIFE makes in three foundational ways: confidence, consistency, and stability. I have emphasized these three preparations for the past thirty years. This book, however, looks at them—especially in terms of God's gospel intent to bring his LIFE to every human life believing in his Son, Jesus Christ. This additional perspective became a necessity in my own life.

. . . .

CHAPTER 3

CONFIDENCE
WITHOUT A WOBBLE

B ABIES BEGIN WALKING with a wobble. They move along with a little support from family and friends. Lacking confidence, they depend on their attachment to others. In those early stages, babies are fine as long as they keep moving. When they stop, they drop. Where they are, that's where they stay, not sure they want to get up again.

Many Christians begin their new walk with Jesus having such a wobble. If they stop, they drop, a little insecure in their efforts. Most of those occasions, as with babies, have to do with an attachment to their previous lives of security and comfort.

A wobble is inevitable. We wobble before we win, stumble before we succeed. A group of tourists visited a village in Europe. They saw an elderly villager and asked, "Have any great people been born here?" The old man, with a twinkle in his eye, said, "Nope, only babies."[14] We have to walk through the wobble stage before we can move on in our dream-walk with Jesus. The questions become, How long will we wobble? How can we get past the wobble in our faith? How can we gain confidence? How can we get past previous comfort zones? The apostle John was faced with such questions.

JOHN, HIS WOBBLE, AND JESUS

John's comfort zone consisted of Jewish, Greek, local, national, work-related and family-related patterns of living. As long as John leaned on them, his walk with Jesus would be more of a wobble than a confident clasping of God's dream to his heart. Normal life-centered living had to change. Until John understood this, his walk with Jesus would be a wobble. The same proves true for us. The only thing that can get us beyond a confidence based on life-centered living is a shift to LIFE-centered living. That is exactly the new possibility that Jesus offered to John, and the new possibility he still offers to us.

Appearing to all the apostles on the day of his resurrection, Jesus challenged each one to accept the LIFE now available to them.

> On the evening of that first day of the week, when the disciples were together, with the doors locked for fear of the Jews, Jesus came and stood among them and said, "Peace be with you!" After he said this, he showed them his hands and side. The disciples were overjoyed when they saw the Lord. Again Jesus said, "Peace be with you! As the Father has sent me, I am sending you." And with that he breathed on them and said, "Receive the Holy Spirit."
>
> —John 20:19-22

What started as a shocking appearance, a common greeting, and a personal demonstration, became a sacred appointment and a new possibility. Alive in the resurrection power of endless LIFE, Jesus breathed on them all.[15] That breath was not the mere exhalation of air; it was the energizing of eternity,[16] the breath of LIFE.

Consider the apostle John. He had been previously awakened. His reflection had brought new understanding, a challenge to his previous way of thinking, and a new grasp of his genuine need. Now came this strange behavior of the Lord when he appeared to his disciples. Now this breath upon his life and this message: "Receive the Holy Spirit." Here was a chance for John to walk differently. Did he do so? No, he wobbled.

John's wobble was evident even in his actions before Christ's appearance to the apostles. When first told of Jesus' post-resurrection appearance to Mary Magdalene and the other women (Mark 16:9ff), John broke off his mourning long enough to ridicule their report. Wobble. Jesus rebuked the apostles for their disbelief and stubbornness.

The need was clear again when John spent forty days with Jesus after the Resurrection—but still missed the point of God's gospel dream for every believer (Acts 1:1-5). He observed the Ascension, but was flabbergasted more than moved (Acts 1:7-12; Luke 24:52-53). Wobble. Then he joined others in an upper room in Jerusalem to pray (Acts 1:13-14), but also to hide. In all this, we see a man beginning a new walk with Jesus but still lacking confidence because of previous life-centered experiences with its perks, lifestyle, and ways of life that did not encourage change. A lingering familiarity with those experiences compromised John's walk.

Why did John wobble? I believe it was due to his previous ways of thinking. He heard the Lord's words, but he still filtered them through previous thought patterns. He had not yet internalized them. He believed in the Resurrection, but he was not yet inspired. Awakened, he knew the truth—but he had not yet been anointed with that truth.

Even the breath of LIFE and Christ's clear pronouncement, "Receive the Holy Spirit," did not bring about instant change. Jesus had told John and the others beforehand that they would receive the Holy Spirit (John 14:15-16). Those words, however, came with a warning:

> The world cannot accept him, because it neither sees him nor knows him. But you know him, for he lives with you and will be in you.
>
> —John 14:17

Nothing in the world could prepare them for what was about to happen.

Perhaps John could not relate the Holy Spirit to LIFE. The dominant religious grid in his life left John with no way of accounting for the Holy Spirit, the very LIFE of God, dwelling in human life as Jesus had declared. The Lord's promise about remaining in the Vine (John 15:1-5) and his pronouncement about receiving the Holy Spirit (John 20:19-22) just didn't fit the apostle's previous structure of interpretation. John was still a blind man walking, and he missed both the Lord's promise and pronouncement.

John could only relate the Spirit's coming to a worldly induced religious experience. He missed the inspired sacred intention of eternity. Jesus had said, "Because I live, you also will live" (John 14:19b). And again, "On that day you will realize that I am in my Father, and you are in me, and I am in you" (John 14:20). Still, John could not see the reality of God's dream in his own life.

Stunned by the LIFE-in-life reality of Jesus Christ at the Resurrection, John was not yet aware that he had been sanctified by the presence of God's LIFE in his own life. As a result, nothing happened in John's life, and for fifty days of uncertainty his walk was characterized by a wobble.

Because of our own blindness and dependence on religious frameworks, we also miss God's gospel promise of his indwelling presence today.

> 6. Does your experience of the Holy Spirit rest on the uniqueness of God's LIFE or on a previous pattern of religious life? Explain if you can. If not, go on.

LOOKING AT OUR OWN WOBBLES

Is it possible that some Christians never get beyond the wobble stage of their walk with Jesus? Do they have a tendency, like John, to maintain previous patterns of understanding for their confidence and security? Do old ways of thinking prevent a full embrace of the new way of thinking that is possible in Christ?

We may have head knowledge about the LIFE of God in Christ, but have no place for that LIFE in our hearts. Perhaps we can reflect on how things ought to be by that LIFE, but miss out on getting there. We may even receive the Spirit but miss his practical application to our lives. Also, we may have never experienced God's complete forgiveness as we continue to struggle with past habits and sins. We may have been poorly introduced to the gospel as part of a religion, a church's expectation, or a denominational explanation—making us miss God's dream altogether. Well-intentioned people may have poorly handled our faith, repentance, confession, and baptism. We easily wobble in doubts and confusion.

For some, fears rise, causing confidence to lag. People avoid walking in the way that God has made possible for them. They walk with Jesus, but fail to walk like Jesus. Some fear they will fall short of expectations, whether their own or those of others. Wobbly fears grow into giant memories and invisible traveling companions. They push aside God's possibilities in us. Sometimes they put their label instead of God's LIFE-in-life dream on the pages of history. Experts have identified more than seventy-five fears, but the biggest confidence-buster is the fear of failure. A person in the fear cycle, says John Maxwell, displays negative side effects that result in further uncertainty:[17]

> *Self-pity.* He feels sorry for himself. And as time goes on, he takes less responsibility for his inactivity and starts thinking of himself as a victim. *Excuses.* A person can fall down many times, but won't be a failure until he says that somebody pushed him. In fact, the person who makes a mistake and then offers an excuse for it adds a second mistake to his first. A person can break out of the fear cycle only by taking personal responsibility for his inaction. *Misused energy.* Constant fear divides the mind and causes a person to lose focus. If he is going in too many directions at once, he doesn't get anywhere. It's comparable to stomping the gas pedal of a car that's in neutral.

Many are like the apostle John during his forty post-resurrection days with Jesus and his ten additional days before Pentecost. John's dreams of leadership and influence were crushed, and he was still blind to God's liberating dream. Like John, we often lack the confidence available to us as we continue to walk with Jesus. We are walking, but wobbling. How do we get past such conditions and move on to confidence?

> 7. Reflect upon your own walk with Jesus, either in previous days or now, and, if possible, identify poor information, limited obedience, fears, self-pity, excuses, and misused energy that have hampered your confidence while walking with Jesus.

REACHING A NEW LEVEL OF CONFIDENCE

The road to confidence is not straight. Adapting an unknown author's words, we can say:

> There is a loop called failure…
> A curve called confusion…
> Red lights called doubts…
> Speed bumps called enemies…
> Flats called friends…
> And caution lights all along the way.

Worldly Advice

The world's advice for achieving confidence appears everywhere. The world admires success and rewards the super-confident. I will describe some of this worldly advice in order to point out the completely different approach to confidence that God provides.

The world's advice centers around five traits reportedly needed for outstanding confidence.[18]

First, the world says those who desire to be confident need to practice *single-minded pragmatism*. A large amount of common sense is needed. People must stick to what works for them and avoid all else. Without apology, they must aim at high standards, value success, leadership, status, and money, while not being bothered too much by things like loyalty and honor.

Second, the world says that confidence-seekers need to depend on *solitary self-reliance*. They must take care of themselves and not let others hold them back. They must become self-starters who love to dream their own dreams and stay light on their feet, able to move on if necessary, to jump at new opportunities. They usually have no problem with certain results of worldly-mindedness that others may find questionable.

In the face of the numbers, varieties, and intensities of modern relationships,[19] they can justify self-protection. Too much involvement with others means unnecessary risks. They are told to "minimize risks, spread the risks, balance the risks, reduce the risks, don't run the risks, don't become risk-prone, and be risk-averse."[20]

Saturated with a plethora of daily contacts with a wide variety of people, most of whom are strangers; the world encourages a self-reliance able to be satisfied with shallow relationships that are trite, superficial, and inconsequential. Conversations and appointments need to be short and hurried—utilitarian in nature. Those who depend on solitary self-reliance are always asking, "What's in it for me?" When connections lose their usefulness, relationships need to be brought to an end. According to this worldly advice, we should expect short-term and interrupted relationships. Life-long connections are not a first priority.

For those depending on self-reliance, the world's advice centers on insincerity. It becomes another feature of worldly wisdom that need not bother the self-reliant. Go ahead and ask, "How are you?" but don't expect an answer because there is no time for a full reply. A newspaper columnist provides worldly advice: "Don't tell everybody your problems—one-third won't listen, another third won't care, and the rest have more problems than you have."[21]

Constant travel and competing interests result in broken, short-term commitments. Suck it up. That's the cost of a confident lifestyle. Focused loyalty brings only collateral damage. Get away from it all by flights of fancy through the electronic media or by real flights using cars, buses, trains, and planes. If relationships don't work out as desired, move on.

Third, those who want to be confident people in the world need to be *self-challenging*. Go ahead and handle tasks that seem just a little too big, or a bit scary—jobs that stretch you to the limit of your abilities. Accept challenges in order to achieve more, challenges that test your intelligence, judgment, skill, or endurance. It's all about success and the pursuit of your own dreams. The moment a task ceases to be challenging, move on to an assignment on the next-higher level. Remaining comfortable with the status quo is no option.

Fourth, confident people in the world are characterized as those who have *personal convictions*. Keenly aware of their environment, they prefer to see it for themselves instead of accepting what others tell them. They want no part of superficial programs, plans, and projects. They tend not to trust others and often have to be convinced that others are not naively mistaken. Needless to say, such qualities will not endear such confidence-seekers to others. But that's the cost of success.

Fifth, confidence-seekers need *a sense of pre-eminence*. Confident people need to see themselves as superior to others in selected qualities like intellect, toughness, and staying power. They need a positive self-image and high self-esteem. A little bit of self-assertiveness, even if unpopular, must be seen in the truly confident. They make decisions quickly, cleanly, and forcefully— and they commit strongly to each decision once it is made. They also work at the skill of convincing others what is right. Those with a sense of pre-eminence dare to believe that their decisions are categorically better than all others.

In case you haven't noticed, all this advice is life-centered. That is to be expected from the world. This kind of advice provides the human dimensions of confidence that too many Christians can easily lean upon. Doing so, they will continue to wobble in comfort zones provided by the world and miss out on the dream-walk with Jesus. Paul saw the dangers of worldly advice and provided an inspired response:

Therefore, I urge you, brothers, in view of God's mercy, to offer your bodies as living sacrifices, holy and pleasing to God—this is your spiritual act of worship. Do not conform any longer to the pattern of this world, but be transformed by the renewing of your mind. Then you will be able to test and approve what God's will is—his good, pleasing and perfect will.

—Rom. 12:1-2

> **8.** In what ways, if any, has the advice from worldly confidence in this section of the book influenced you?

Life-centered confidence that depends on our dreams contrasts sharply with LIFE-centered confidence that depends on God's dream lived out in our lives. John began to see this contrast in Jesus.

The Lord's Steadfast Walk of Confidence

John's confidence at a LIFE-centered level finally occurred on the day of Pentecost after fifty days of wobbling belief. The promised power of the Holy Spirit came upon him and the others. "But you will receive power when the Holy Spirit comes on you; and you will be my witnesses in Jerusalem, and in all Judea and Samaria, and to the ends of the earth" (Acts 1:8). What happened after the Holy Spirit descended on the day of Pentecost can be reviewed in the second chapter of Acts. Strange sights, sounds, and power. All linked with the new presence of the unifying LIFE of Father, Son, and Holy Spirit.

Now John began seeing the impact of that LIFE upon human life when the Holy Spirit of God's LIFE comes to dwell in the lives of people. No mere transformation of John's old life was sufficient for God's dream. Only the transfusion of God's own LIFE according to the eternal plan adequately portrayed the dream. LIFE worked from within, not just from without.

In further reflection on his three years with the Lord, the apostle John may now have seen how Jesus had walked a confident

LIFE-in-life way in God's eternal dream. Born as a man, he bore the life of humankind. Born of a virgin, he bore the LIFE of God. Obedient to earthly parents, he honoured the Father and grew in wisdom, stature, and favor—in all ways pleasing to both God and men (Luke 2:49-52). Human life and divine LIFE blended perfectly in the Lord, and he was confident in both.

Walking among the people of his day, Jesus grieved at their desperation, helped them struggle with human ignorance, welcomed their association, attended to their health, fought against their fears, and confronted their sins. He saw them wobble, totter, and flounder for lack of confidence, but he never slowed the pace of his dream-walk. He fully identified with life but never forgot who he was and what he had. He bore life *and* LIFE. His was a LIFE-in-life walk of confidence.

John and the other disciples had initially missed the significance of Christ's LIFE-in-life confidence. Blessed by Christ's companionship, they were still bound to the frail conditions of human life alone. They resembled the crowds, not Jesus. Blinded by natural circumstances, worried, powerless, and impatient in the crowds of their day, they missed LIFE even when Jesus walked with them.

The contrast between Jesus and the disciples must have convicted John later in his life. Three instances in the fifth chapter of Luke illustrate Jesus and the crowds. In the first verse, Jesus took advantage of a nearby boat to continue instructing a crowd. In verses fifteen and sixteen he ministered to the crowds and then withdrew to a lonely place to pray. In verse nineteen the crowd around him was so tightly packed that some men on a desperate mission to save their paralyzed companion climbed onto a roof and lowered the man into his presence. Crowds surrounded him again in Luke 8:19-21 and 9:10-11. In Luke 9:37, a large crowd met him at the base of a mountain, and in Luke 12:1, a crowd numbering in the thousands trampled on each other to see the Lord.

In all these circumstances, Jesus remained confidently patient, available, focused, and servant-like. But the disciples, including

John, lost sympathy for individuals in the teeming crowds (Luke 8:45), saw no feasible way to meet basic needs (9:12-13), and were lividly impatient with opportunists among the people (18:15-17). Self-protective, avoiding risk, superficially present, utilitarian, insincere, cynical, distrusting, lacking commitment—the worldly patterns of their time were probably similar to ours. The disciples were with Jesus, but were still wobbling in uncertainty.

For John, it was time to walk like Jesus. It was time to realize that the LIFE he had was the LIFE they had been given, too. God's LIFE was the basis of a deep, strong confidence. Deep, not by a greater intensity of life, but by the confident presence of LIFE. Strong, not by increased human activity, but by God's presence in his life.

> **9.** Based on your previous walk with Jesus, how confident would you say you have been about your time with Jesus. Score yourself on a scale of 1 to 10, with 1 being none at all, and 10 being complete. Record and explain your score in your journal. How can this study help move your score ahead?

THE SACRED DIMENSION OF DISCIPLESHIP

LIFE within was the sacred dimension of discipleship that had been lacking in John's walk with the Lord. Absent during the three-year sojourn, absent during the forty-day post-resurrection appearances, absent during the ten secretive days in the upper room—LIFE within for John finally appeared with power on the day of Pentecost. Confusion gave way to confidence. Doubts gave way to courage. Life-centered inactivity gave way to LIFE-centered activity. Excuses gave way to exaltation. Fear gave way to faith. Wobble gave way to a powerful LIFE-centered way forward. Confidence is the element we all need to be dream-walkers like Jesus.

John's change at this level of confidence can be related to the number of times he uses the word *confidence* in his epistles. Some examples are:

And now, dear children, continue in him, so that when he appears we may be confident and unashamed before him at his coming.

—1 John 2:28

Dear friends, if our hearts do not condemn us, we have confidence before God.

—1 John 3:21

In this way, love is made complete among us so that we will have confidence on the day of judgment, because in this world we are like him.

—1 John 4:17

We, too, can become such dream-walkers. Our wobble can be replaced by the strength of God's abiding presence. The kind of confidence that gets up whenever life knocks us down can begin to surface from our faith—going not to our heads but to Christ's feet.[22]

I came to this level of confidence belatedly in my efforts at discipleship mobilization. The original discipleship books had the right idea. They explored John's foundational ingredients of confidence as revealed in his gospel and epistles. They emphasized the certainty of belonging to the family of God (John 1:12-13), of having new life (John 5:24; 1 John 2:25), and of realizing the new presence of the Holy Spirit in our lives (1 John 3:24, 4:13). But they lacked the substance that held these three necessities together.

I soon learned it was not enough to gather the elements the way a builder gathers the tools, sand, rock, and cement for a foundation. It was necessary to combine these elements in a power-binding way. For the builder, water was essential for the bonding. For the disciple, God's LIFE is like that water, flowing in, around, and through every element of our Christian experience.

Relationships, new beginnings, and even new promises are inadequate alone. These three without the ingredient of LIFE may help us to conform but cannot help us to be confident LIFE-in-life people. They can point to the kind of confidence we need, but they cannot point to the power behind that confidence. We all need LIFE to stand confidently on the foundations of discipleship. Unless we gain such confidence, there is little reason to go on and seek LIFE-centered consistency, which is our topic in the next chapter.

CHAPTER 4

. . . .

DREAM-WALKING
CONSISTENCY

BABIES SOON BECOME walkers and thrill us with their progress as they move from step to more confident step. Sometimes they move too quickly for tired mothers and anxious fathers. Disciplined consistency comes into the picture when it becomes clear to parents that when babies start walking, they have to be followed with instructions: "No, don't touch that." "Stop, don't go there." "Wait, that's hot!" It is no surprise that one of the first words babies learn is *no*.

Some babies keep testing the boundaries. With thoughtful looks on their little faces, some obey while others disobey. We have all seen that mischievous look that seems to say, "Are you going to follow me? How fast can you get to where I'm going?" Some babies pitch fits, while others are easily distracted by another activity. Moods change rapidly. Babies need to learn to navigate, and they need discipline and direction.

Discipline gives some people the impression of restriction, routine, regimentation, and constraint. Some parents have disciplined their toddlers like that. But a better understanding of discipline is expressed in words like *trained, cultivated, refined,* and *developed.* If we do not discipline children correctly, what we get is the opposite of discipline: unmanageable kids who are out of control, wild, disobedient, willful, and disruptive. Some disobedient behavior is inevitable as children explore their new independence while lacking language and social skills. I just googled "the terrible twos," and I got 282,000 results.

Our two sons—now young adults—like to comment on the methods we used with them. The older is reminded every time someone snaps his fingers; that was my way of training a young walker. The younger has observed the tantrums of children in public, turned to his mother, and said, "Mom, give that child your look." Training and refinement worked with our kids.

Disciples also need discipline and direction. Otherwise they may become walkers, but they risk missing the dream-walk that is possible with Jesus. Like toddlers, they can be walking in a good direction, and then suddenly become distracted to a lesser goal. At such times, we all benefit from having our walks defined and being given some direction. "The greatest thing in the world," said Oliver Wendell Holmes, "is not so much where we stand as in what direction we're moving."[23]

Some Christians resist this blessing of dream-walking consistency. They balk at discipline and run from direction. For the slightest reason they take off on new tracks with all kinds of things stimulating and distracting them. They make their own plans, chase their own dreams, and challenge God to follow after them.

---

10. "Many make their own plans, chase their own dreams, and ask a *doting God* to simply chase after them." Reflect on your past walk with Jesus. Does this sentence describe you in any way at any time?

Discipline is important to the dream-walk.

My first thirty years of discipleship work were devoted to bringing greater consistency to Christian lives. Using John's gospel and epistles, I developed six familiar areas of discipline: Bible study, prayer, fellowship, confession, giving, and fruitfulness. I still maintain their importance. Reflecting on my methods, however, I realize they were strong on discipline but weak on *direction*. If anything, my direction was more of a design than a dream, and I soon learned that human discipline without divine direction does not get one very far. It depends too much on the essential disciplines of life without the energetic direction of LIFE. The "rut of routine" alone never becomes the "groove of grace," as Vernon Grounds put it.[24]

How can discipline and direction be combined in dream-walking discipleship for strong foundations in training Christ's followers?

JOHN'S SHAKY FOUNDATION

As we have seen, John was a man of his world. The life-centered patterns of that world greatly influenced him, even when he followed Jesus for three years. He was influenced again after the Resurrection and before the day of Pentecost. We have to wonder how John struggled beyond crawling and scooting, beyond the one step or two, and if he went through anything like the terrible twos. The Bible does not tell us, but I would like to propose a scenario.

John still had personal issues to face beyond Pentecost. He needed the further discipline and direction of consistency. Perhaps this is the place to recall that one of his aims during the ministry of Jesus was to sit at Christ's right hand, with his brother on the left. John was overly ambitious. He wanted to be considered a real leader. And that was the wrong direction.

> Then the mother of Zebedee's sons came to Jesus with her sons and, kneeling down, asked a favor of him. "What is it you want?" he asked. She said, "Grant that one of these two sons of mine may sit at your right and the other at your left in your kingdom." "You don't know what you are asking," Jesus said to them. "Can you drink the cup I am going to drink?" "We can," they answered. Jesus said to them, "You will indeed drink from my cup, but to sit at my right or left is not for me to grant. These places belong to those for whom they have been prepared by my Father." When the ten heard about this, they were indignant with

the two brothers. Jesus called them together and said, "You know that the rulers of the Gentiles lord it over them, and their high officials exercise authority over them. Not so with you. Instead, whoever wants to become great among you must be your servant, and whoever wants to be first must be your slave—just as the Son of Man did not come to be served, but to serve, and to give his life as a ransom for many."

—Matt. 20:20-28; also Mark 10:35-45

Initially, John was a man with his own plans and dreams—and he wanted the LIFE-giver to bless him. He was still crawling at this time in his walk with the Lord, but he crawled with purpose and resolve. Some of that same personal drive may have followed him into his later discipleship. The Bible does not tell us, but there was probably a time when he was like a two-year old, going where he wanted, testing the boundaries, and thinking others should follow and support him.

John was far from being a dream-walker. As we see in Matthew 20, John would have to learn that the issue was not leadership—going where he wanted and getting others to follow him. Jesus confronted John with another topic altogether: *fellowship*. To Jesus, fellowship was more important than leadership. Big contrast. Jesus offered the cup of fellowship, not the crown of leadership. He extended the cup of suffering, not the crown of success. Jesus offered a fellowship defined by the qualities of God's LIFE, not human life.

The transformations in John's life came at the Resurrection and after the secretive days in the upper room. That is when LIFE-in-life possibilities became a reality for him. John had previously been distracted from God's interest in fellowship due to his own interest in human leadership. Now, John would have to yield to the fellowship that provides a strong foundation for the sharing of Christlikeness, evangelism, and discipling that are part of discipleship mobilization.

Before we look more carefully at the apostle John's journey of consistency, we need to pay some attention to our own distractions. What keeps us from dream-walking consistency today?

The World's Distractions

As Christians we may not be distracted by leadership ambitions like John, but the world offers many other temptations. In yielding to these, we also miss the possibilities of dream-walking with Jesus. Confronted with the choice of discipline and direction—or distraction, we often choose to be distracted by the world's enticements. Like toddlers loving their new mobility, our attention is easily diverted by nine temptations of today's world: (1) knowledge, (2) visual images, (3) spectacle, (4) entertainment, (5) relativism, (6) suspicion of authority, (7) impermanent values, (8) pluralism, and (9) uncertainty.[25] All of these distractions disturb consistency.

Life-centered Knowledge

Life-centered knowledge easily distracts Christians. See it, chase it, get it. The world eagerly offers knowledge as the ultimate end for most of us. Books, courses, seminars, Web sites, conferences, institutions, and organizations—all offer that all-important knowledge. The number of books published each year must be astronomical. In the USA alone, something like sixty thousand books will appear. The electronic world and mass media add to this dizzying expansion of knowledge. Thoughts, symbols, arguments, viewpoints, issues, proposals, and plans turn over at accelerating rates. Worldwide knowledge is multiplied four to five times every ten years. "The newest is the truest and the latest is the greatest,"[26] says the modern maxim. What results do we find from the pursuit of knowledge?

- Insecure in a *simple* kind of knowledge, we often question the validity and worthiness of our Christian stance.
- Increasingly dependent on knowledge couched in science, technology, academia, and professional expertise, we become less reliant on God and fail to relate all knowledge to him.
- Severed from our faith, wisdom, and action, our knowledge results in fuzzy thinking and faddish feelings.

Such results hinder disciplined consistency and leave Christians like toddlers, easily distracted by this and that.

Visual Images

Television, computers, laptops, cell-phones, I-Pods—they all broadcast a flurry of images that change our ways of thinking. Television and the Internet set the standards of rapidly changing images, fleeting glimpses, simplicity, and diverse thoughts that never slow down and give pause to reflect. These visual mechanisms inform but do not involve the watcher. They result in less mental processing, reasoning, substance, and reality. Reducing the length of time one is able to concentrate, they focus on superficiality, surface impressions, fragmented information, and subjectivity. Absurdity plays with our minds. What are the results?

- Visual symbols dominate our Christian landscape and are upheld as *spiritual*; verbal symbols, the basis of discipleship consistency, are belittled as *boring*.
- We become watchers instead of walkers, judging the performances of others instead of implementing our own under Christ's Lordship.
- We measure everything by sight and are left with visual impressions lacking depth and substance.

Constant access to visual images hinders the possibilities of a consistent walk with Jesus.

Christian Spectacle

Things that are eye-catching in today's world are measured by the standards of the television and movie screen. It is spectacle. These media make the greens greener, the reds redder, everything larger, actions faster, and all things more interesting—all playing to our need for dramatic sensation. Media life is made to look even more alive—causing us to wonder if we are really living as we could. Tempo, sound, and sight increase, causing us to become uncomfortable and disinterested in anything lower or slower. Then surface feelings become the things that appeal to us: looks, touch, scents, and sounds. "Substance is unimportant, style is what

counts," says Os Guinness describing this feature in America.[27]
The result?

- We stop implementing the basics (like Bible reading) and are drawn instead to experiential events and charismatic leaders.
- Worship itself becomes a life-centered spectacle, with churches expending large amounts of money to set the stage and use the latest electronic technology.
- Emotional involvement becomes the test of authenticity as other realms of personality are ignored. Spiritual maturity is hindered by lopsided attention to the sensual.
- As Os Guinness observed, "Who we are takes second place to…who we appear to be."[28]

Disciplined consistency sounds dull in such hyped-up atmospheres.

Spiritual Entertainment

In today's world, its level of enjoyment, pleasure, and recreation measures everything. George Barna's research shows that in the United States, "three out of every five adults (61 percent) agreed that 'the main purpose of life is enjoyment and personal fulfillment.'" What may be most disturbing, said the Christian researcher, is that "half of all born-again Christians (50 percent) and more than one-third of all evangelicals (37 percent) believe that life's purpose is enjoyment and self-satisfaction."[29] If it sounds good, believe it. If it feels good, do it. Performance and pretence dominate much of Christian communication. While only one in ten people pay any attention to a speaker's content; four evaluate his appearance, and the rest measure the person's style and delivery. Theater prevails over thought. What is the result?

- We become driven by outward expectations of entertainment excellence; discipleship appears very drab in the face of all this *excitement*.

- We don't have time for the things of God because much of our time is spent in the pursuit of pleasure and the things that provide it.
- Consistency based on discipline and direction is not perceived as enjoyable or fun.

> **11.** Before going further, reflect upon these first four ingredients of today's world. Do you see them as distractions to discipleship consistency of Bible reading, prayer, fellowship, confession of Christ's name, giving and fruitfulness in your life? If so, how?

Everything is Relative

Knowledge and values are not absolute, according to today's world; they are relative to a person's nature and situation. George Barna discovered that in the USA "three-quarters of all adults (72 percent) agreed that 'there is no such thing as absolute truth; two people could define truth in totally conflicting ways, but both could still be correct.' A similar percentage claimed that 'When it comes to morals and ethics ... there are no absolute standards that apply to everybody in all situations.' ... People are more likely today to reject absolute truth than they are to accept its existence."[30] Even discipleship consistency becomes relative, along with discipline and direction. What results come about?

- The climate of relativism and tolerance makes many Christians apologetic and confused about a firm biblical base of absolutes, permanent values, and certainty that point to consistency.
- We are increasingly tempted to live without consistent standards in the midst of relativistic morals and values, turning *consistency* elsewhere into hypocrisy.

There is No Authority

Knowledge and values are seen through the eyes of six billion people today, making everyone's view different and justifiable. We live in a day that amplifies ambiguities, distorts truth, and buries reality under diverse and contrasting opinions. Conferences, conventions, and consultations piece together the ideas of "experts" while citizens do whatever seems right to attain *worthy* goals. Unchanging truth is suspect. In fact, unchanging truth does not exist, so who can be sure of anything? Tradition is questioned and leadership is disdained even though competing life-centered authorities seek to have the last word. What are the results for consistency?

- We are suspicious of Christian leadership.
- Biblical authority is lost to the prevailing interpretations of leaders.
- Human models become the object of religious devotion, and we often assume that respect for a man or ministry is equivalent to our respect for God.
- Our churches and organizations keep shifting their message and methods.

In such an environment, someone's consistency may be interpreted as religious legalism or cult submission.

There Are No Permanent Values

Pure, unblemished certainties do not exist in today's life-driven world. When everything is relative, there are no permanent values to live by. Politicians busily redefine everything in their parliaments, congresses, conferences, committees, and commissions because God's absolutes and values are denied. Lobbying groups have a heyday. Experts become the high priests of the new climate that excludes God. Good is valued for the sake of good itself, and bad depends on many personal factors, such as where we come from, how we have lived, and the opportunities we have been given. Love, generosity, goodness, submission, gentleness, sympathy, mercy—all these things become mushy and without substance, except as different situations call for them. Permanent values shatter as politically correct efforts are made to equalize all that is deemed either good or evil. The big question is whether we shall do the lesser evil or the greater good. The results for consistency?

- We seek life-centered consensus in our own group of believers rather than God-centered biblical authority.
- Some band together with like-minded people in "holy huddles" for familiarity and protection, becoming isolated while finding happiness in a small circle.
- It becomes common to be blindly loyal to a group, individual, church, choir, or some such network offering security and a sense of belonging.

Consistency based on God's permanent values is minimized.

Pluralism

Pluralism is the accepted standard in today's world—the plurality of opinions, values, ethnicity, religions, and cultural experiences. We are faced with too many choices, a chaos of competing interests, necessities and opportunities. The result?

- Pluralism weakens our interest in anything like a singular journey toward consistency.
- The very image of Christian associations like the church constantly change according to diverse standards, activities, and expectations.
- Continuity of purpose and direction suffers.
- Commitment diminishes in time as well as intensity. The temptation is to know only enough and care only as necessary.
- A wrong singularity becomes common. Single-mindedness that has a clear focus on God is replaced by a simple-mindedness focused on human association.

We Are Left with Uncertainty

"Yesterday's truth becomes today's fiction," says Os Guinness.[31] "Nothing is certain except death and taxes—and both get you into a hole," says another observer. Many options mean many opinions. How does this affect consistent Christian living?

- It becomes increasingly difficult for Christians to make decisions.
- We learn to distrust anyone who is always so *certain*.

Even descriptions of consistency join the list of our uncertainties.

---

12. For your *Dream-walking Journal*, choose one of the last five features of the modern world and describe how it has distracted you (if relevant) from the disciplines of consistent Bible reading, prayer, fellowship, confession of Christ, giving and fruitfulness.

These nine distractions provide a way to understand our own acceptance of some of the attitudes and behaviors listed above. Modern distractions greatly reduce the possibility of consistency in Christian lives. The list is not all-inclusive; there are certainly other distractions beyond these. The apostle John surely also held many other worldly assumptions in addition to his assumptions about leadership.

The point is that we need to stand against the dominant worldly patterns to experience disciplined consistency in a walk like that of Jesus. As Philip Yancey has said, "The visible world forces itself on [us] without invitation; [we] must consciously cultivate the invisible."[32] How do we do that?

THE SACRED DIMENSIONS OF CONSISTENCY

Having seen how the human dimensions of a worldly kind hinder disciplined Christian consistency, we need to be reminded of the divine dimension that enables it. This sacred dimension was seen in Jesus. It was necessary to John. And it is essential for us today.

47

Christ's Perfect Consistency

Jesus demonstrated a disciplined consistency. For example, he showed astute familiarity with the Scriptures (Matt. 4:1-11; Luke 4:14-27), spent much time in prayer (Luke 6:12, 9:28; John 17:1-26), brought special qualities to fellowship (John 13:3-17), confessed the authority of the Father many times (Matt. 11:27), modeled a generous lifestyle (John 6:1-15), and was fruitful in his service (John 4:4-42). These foundational disciplines were complemented by his submission to the gospel direction of his life—a thirty-three year walk that ended at the cross.

In addition to his discipline and direction, the sacred dimension of LIFE from the Father blessed Jesus. The presence of divine LIFE in his human life made his walk a dream-walk. In other words, Jesus read the Scriptures and meditated on them with a LIFE-in-life energy. For him, prayer was a LIFE-in-life event. Fellowship to him was defined by the LIFE of the Father, a unique meeting of LIFE with life. He never boasted of his life but always acknowledged LIFE as the reason for his actions. When he gave—whether food, healing, instruction, or encouragement—he gave from his LIFE-in-life identity, security, and resources. When he bore fruit, it was always the fruit of LIFE pouring forth from his life.

> 13. Reflect upon your own consistency in the six recommended responses seen even in the life of Jesus. What difference is made (or needs to be made) by the presence of God's LIFE in your life?

John's Transformed Consistency

How did John come to express consistency? A disciplined spiritual walk did become an important part of John's ministry. He wrote, "But if we walk in the light, as he is in the light, we have fellowship with one another, and the blood of Jesus, his Son, purifies us from all sin" (1 John 1:7).

Of the disciplines that Jesus modeled, I think John was most amazed by the LIFE Jesus showed in fellowship. That is why the

Lord offered John and his disciples fellowship instead of leadership (Matt. 20:13-20). That fellowship was based on the presence of LIFE in those who belong to the family of God. Attention to the Word of God, prayer, confession, giving, and fruitfulness all rose out of the fellowship.

In LIFE-centered fellowship there was a LOVE that John could not ignore, which became a central thrust later in his message and ministry. He changed from an intolerant, narrow-minded disciple confined to life's conditional loves, to one filled with LIFE's unconditional LOVE. The apostle knew about romantic love (*eros*) and relational love (*phileo*), but Jesus kept using another Greek word for love: *agape*. When agape love is used in the New Testament, it is always connected to God and the good news in Jesus Christ. Once he saw the connection between LIFE and LOVE, John's understanding of relationships was totally revolutionized. His epistles show that he became a man overwhelmed by this LOVE. He wrote, "This is how we know what love is: Jesus Christ laid down his life for us" (1 John 3:16). And he wrote this famous passage about God's love for us:

> Dear friends, let us love one another, for love comes from God. Everyone who loves has been born of God and knows God. Whoever does not love does not know God; because God is love. This is how God showed his love among us: He sent his one and only Son into the world that we might live through him. This is love: not that we loved God but that he loved us and sent his Son as an atoning sacrifice for our sins. Dear friends, since God so loved us, we also ought to love one another. No one has ever seen God; but if we love one another, God lives in us and his love is made complete in us.
>
> We know that we live in him and he in us, because he has given us of his Spirit. And we have seen and testify that the Father has sent his Son to be the Savior of the world. If anyone acknowledges that Jesus is the Son of God, God lives in him and he in God. And so we know and rely on the love God has for us.
>
> God is love, whoever lives in love lives in God, and God in him. In this way love is made complete among us so that we will have confidence on the day of judgment, because in this world

we are like him. There is no fear in love. But perfect love drives out fear, because fear has to do with punishment. The one who fears is not made perfect in love.
We love because he first loved us.

—1 John 4:7-19

In the thirteen verses of that passage, John mentions love twenty-two times. Where there is LIFE, there is always LOVE—*agape,* God's very own LOVE. The old has gone. The new has come. Another way to put this: John's life-centered loves had been superseded by God's LOVE.

---

14. How can your understanding of fellowship be radically changed by the real addition of God's LIFE and His LOVE to your thinking, experience and life?

I believe John became fixated on LIFE and LOVE with its fellowship of discipline and direction. He wrote as a LIFE-in-life man transformed to a consistency of fellowship that influenced every other discipline and the direction of his discipleship walk with Jesus. He shifted from his focus on leadership to the Lord's focus on fellowship, and that fellowship became the defining message of John's ministry.

That which was from the beginning, which we have heard, which we have seen with our eyes, which we have looked at and our hands have touched—this we proclaim concerning the Word of life. The life appeared; we have seen it and testify to it, and we proclaim to you the eternal life, which was with the Father and has appeared to us. We proclaim to you what we have seen and heard, so that you also may have fellowship with us. And our fellowship is with the Father and with his Son, Jesus Christ.

—1 John 1:1-3

This is the message we have heard from him and declare to you: God is light; in him there is no darkness at all. If we claim to have fellowship with him yet walk in the darkness, we lie and do not live by the truth. But if we walk in the light, as he is in the light, we have fellowship with one another, and the blood of Jesus, his Son, purifies us from all sin.

—1 John 1:5-7

After some time, John became known as a *pillar* of the church (Gal. 2:9). He was supportive, helpful, and protective of others. He had learned the importance of a servant-fellowship that outshines even our current interest in servant-leadership. He had been transformed.

Our Response to the Challenge

There will be no dream-walking consistency in our lives until we are transformed on the inside, as was John. We must turn away from worldly patterns of living. We cannot walk consistently if we continue living so distractedly. We must turn to the sacred pattern demonstrated by Jesus, learned by John, and so essential to us.

In turning from worldly ways, we do not just choose some new religious ways for the disciplines of Bible reading, prayer, fellowship, confession, giving, and fruitfulness. Instead, we turn to LIFE's presence and prompting in our lives. We do not replace one set of life-centered ways with a new set of life-centered ways. For the Christian, the dream-walk with Jesus takes us far beyond life-centered ways. Everything becomes LIFE-centered.

LIFE-centered ways open up new avenues of attitude, thought, and behaviour about all the disciplines. The sacred dimension of discipleship takes us in new directions as we walk *with* God, not just *for* God.

Where can we begin? Perhaps, like John, we need to begin with a new understanding of fellowship defined in terms of God's LIFE in our lives and the lives of those with whom we seek consistency. His very LIFE in us, not just a religious belief about him, is the basis of such consistency. Perhaps Bible reading, prayer, the confession of Christ, giving, or fruitfulness will be the starter. Whichever discipline gets us moving as dream-walkers, expect new energy and resolve. This is dream-walking.

51

For me, the change came in Bible reading. God's LIFE in my life created a new hunger for his LIFE-in-life word. That hunger has affected all the other disciplines. Prayer has become LIFE-in-life times, and fellowship is now based on recognition of its special quality when people share LIFE. Bringing Jesus into my conversations is always a prompting of LIFE in my life, and giving is no longer just a giving of my life, but a giving of LIFE-in-life resources.

No rut of routine for me; the groove of grace has come. That groove is available to all. In fact, it will be necessary, because routine will not take us through suffering (our next topic of consideration), but grace will.

> **15**. Discipleship needs fellowship for consistency. How can you find or form a group of disciples engaged with you in dream-walking consistency?

CHAPTER 5

. . . .

LIFE'S STABILITY FOR
LIFE'S SUFFERING

A S OUR CHILDREN get on their feet and start conquering the world, the number of spills, banged knees, bumped foreheads, loosened teeth, and myriad other accidents multiply. We offer comfort, solace, Band-Aids, lessons, and encouragement. One night, a four-year-old was going home from church with his Aunt Ilene. He reflected a bit on the important lessons he had learned in church that day and said, "I wish I could live my life over again." Perhaps some of those spills and banged knees were just too much. His aunt fondly remembers the moment.

As disciples, we are going to have our spills and banged knees. We will need stability to emerge from the inevitable suffering and go on walking. We will not be able to live life over again. The human dimensions of suffering may suffocate and break us in the depths of despair, but the sacred dimension of stability will steer us to new heights of blessing. The world, operating from the limits of human life, may offer suffering like a thick darkness, but God from his infinite LIFE will offer stability like a brilliant light. That is our opportunity to become dream-walkers.

DISCIPLESHIP AND LIFE'S SUFFERING

In my early efforts to add stability into the foundations of discipleship, I broadened the scope of suffering to include temptation, doubt, sorrow, conflicts, and even false teaching. Sorrow was not the lone contender, as often presumed. Each addition brings darkened suffering to a disciple's life.

> **16.** As you read the descriptions of suffering below, circle significant words that describe your own times of suffering, relate one or two to your own experience in your *Journal*.

- Temptations to wrong behavior, attitudes, and the pursuit of power, pleasure, position, prosperity, possessions, and pride result in the suffering of self-doubts, disgust, shame, guilt, disloyalty, dishonesty, deception, secrecy, selfishness, carelessness, and foolishness.
- Doubts include those about ourselves and about God. We doubt abilities, our esteem, salvation, forgiveness, honesty, and ourselves. We become intimidated, frightened, weak, vulnerable, and worried. We doubt God's love, promises, existence, and ability, and we suffer spiritual blindness, dullness of mind, stubbornness, and self-centered limitations.
- Sorrow, though usually related to death and the loss of loved ones, also feeds on the loss of many other things like security, safety, peace, homes, daily provisions, sufficient funds, jobs, opportunities for advancement, belongings, acceptance, friendships, freedom, health, limbs, strength, mobility, innocence, marriage, parents, and family. These losses may cause sadness, misery, pain, loneliness, and a sense of failure, depression, despair, regret, and disappointment.
- Conflict causes sufferings to arise because of broken relationships with spouses, children, parents, friends, employers, co-workers, groups, and Christian associates. What do we become in suffering? We become abandoned,

deserted, fearful, betrayed, defensive, humiliated, distrustful, disappointed, remorseful, losers, failures, angry, stressed, and disillusioned.

- False teaching may seem a strange topic for suffering. This pain arises from the influence of cunning, deceitful, and scheming people, however, leaving us feeling deceived, misled, confused, besieged, manipulated, threatened, and abused.

We can all relate stories to many of the above experiences. During our first thirty years while making disciples and training others to do so, we found evidence for all types of suffering. One man had lost a child; another, his job; a third, his integrity; and a fourth, his wife's support. My wife discipled one woman going through a divorce, another experiencing abuse and violence, and a third struggling as a single mother. All suffered in different ways. Seventy other disciples had their own stories of suffering.

A disciple's suffering is inevitable. Jesus said, "I have told you these things, so that in me you may have peace. In this world you will have trouble" (John 16:33). "Whoever wants to save his life will lose it," he said, "but whoever loses his life for me and for the gospel will save it" (Mark 8:35). Paul warned that "everyone who wants to live a godly life in Christ Jesus will be persecuted, while evil men will go from bad to worse, deceiving and being deceived" (2 Tim. 3:12-13). He called people to join with him "in suffering for the gospel" (2 Tim. 1:8). As Christians, he said, we "groan inwardly as we wait eagerly for adoption as sons, the redemption of our bodies" (Rom. 8:23).[33]

A disciple's suffering can also be instructive. C. H. Spurgeon said, "Great hearts can only be made by great troubles," and "Great faith must have great trials." Calvin Miller has written that "Only the broken bring the flame," and Selwyn Hughes notes, "It's the heart that's afraid of breaking that never learns to dance."[34]

Platitudes? By themselves, perhaps. Behind these brief sentences, however, the authors have seriously examined the topic. That task is left to them, and such books are excellent.[35] Our task here is to examine the impact of suffering on discipleship possibilities. We will look first at the modern experience, and then we will try again to trace John's experience as he learned to be a dream-walker with Jesus after Pentecost.

The Modern Experience

A skewed perspective on suffering dominates many success-driven societies. The manufacturing world scraps suffering and sells comfort. The media exposes suffering and endorses comfort. The health services industry cures suffering and profits from healing. And on and on. So, in the face of modern society, why should we tolerate suffering and support discomfort?

The modern world glorifies health, success, strength and luxury, while avoiding anything resembling weakness in our thinking, behavior, relationships, physique, work and lifestyle. John Piper observes that some believe people deserve a pain-free, trouble-free existence.[36] That is probably why nearly twenty-five percent of the US economy runs through the health industry. Suffering interrupts our health and intrudes on our well-being. Philip Yancey contrasted "valid" and "invalid" to demonstrate an unfortunate attitude. If we are well, comfortable, and at peace, we are valid; if the opposite is true, we are invalid.[37] Discomfort distresses us. The pain of others embarrasses us as we feebly try to encourage, inspire, and soothe. With good intentions, we often say exactly the wrong things: "I know how you feel…" "Don't worry…" "Get well soon…"

Even our more *normal* experiences belie the modern assumption that we can live beyond suffering in a sanitized world:

- When the bills and credit cards finally get paid, and the budget seems in order, the car needs major repairs.
- We manage to meet a deadline at work only to be told of a new set of goals and expectations.
- Selfish and greedy professional financial planners manipulate hard-earned investments.

- We upgrade our career skills only to learn that a younger generation with totally new knowledge and skills has overtaken our chances for advancement.
- We pay exorbitant taxes on fuel, goods, and income, but we watch with dismay as governments find new ways to use more money and seek more taxes.
- We resolve a broken relationship with a work colleague but go home and have a serious conflict with our spouse or children.

"Just when you think you are winning the rat race, along come faster rats," says one bumper sticker.[38] The human dimensions of suffering attack stability. Dissatisfaction with physical appearance, home maintenance demands, lost items, too many tasks, family health problems, the stress that others unload on you, the demands of children, fear for their delinquency, unwanted pregnancies, deaths, illnesses, and job losses—all this suffering darkens discipleship resolve.

> 17. Relate one incident in your life when you thought you were winning "the rat race," only to find "faster rats."

John's Experience of Suffering

Human dimensions hindered John's confidence and consistency. They also attacked his stability. Something was off in his day too. Something like a bad aroma drifted through his life. John needed only to look around to see that something was wrong. Life was hard, cruel, and painful. Things just didn't make sense as he observed temptations, doubts, sorrow, conflicts, and falsehood all around him.

As a Son of Thunder walking with Jesus but not yet dreamwalking, John had a tendency to blow up at life and become impatient with the sick, hungry, troubled, and lost.[39] After the Resurrection, it seemed he had no one with whom to walk, so John withdrew into gloomy human dimensions of suffering. Consider some of his possible feelings during the forty-nine days before Pentecost:

- *Temptation.* There was disgust and shame at his own disloyalty, unreliability, and deception toward the Messiah.
- *Doubt.* There was fear, intimidation, worry, and feelings of weakness and uselessness.
- *Sorrow.* There was sadness, misery, pain, depression, regret, and disappointment.
- *Conflict.* There was remorse, anger, stress, and disillusionment.
- *False Teaching.* There was a sudden vulnerability to powerful religious leaders.

Those feelings, most likely, still rumbled through his life like rolling thunder during the forty-nine days after the resurrection of Christ. Perhaps that is why he went fishing with Peter (John 21:1-3). What would you have done?

Even the power of Pentecost did not remove the presence of pain. The Bible does not specifically describe John, but he had to have been caught up in the troubles of his time. We can trace four such times in the book of Acts, concerning temptation, conflict, falsehood, and sorrow. By seeing the life-centered human dimensions of John's sufferings, we will appreciate the LIFE-centered sacred dimension God brought into John's life—and wants to bring into ours.

Life-centered Temptation

In Acts 3:1-26, John was engaged with Peter in an event centered on a man lame from birth and now more than forty years old (Acts 4:22). The man had begged for money, but Peter healed him instead. The succeeding events offer a possible glimpse at John's suffering.

> While the beggar held on to Peter and John, all the people were astonished and came running to them in the place called Solomon's Colonnade. When Peter saw this, he said to them: "Men of Israel, why does this surprise you? Why do you stare at us as if by our own power or godliness we had made this man walk?
> —Acts 3:11-12

Try to imagine John's temptations as the lame man clung to them. Like us, he may have been tempted to accept the credit, take pride in his evident power and super-spirituality, put God aside for the moment, and exult in a personal victory. These are temptations we still face today whenever God does something special through our lives. John was no different. He was a disciple still learning to dream-walk the way Jesus did.

Life-centered Conflict

The third chapter of Acts ends with Peter speaking to the onlookers at Solomon's Colonnade. But Acts 4:1-22 suggests further sufferings for John. Religious leaders condemned Peter and John for preaching about Jesus, and put them in jail for the night. They interrogated them the next day and warned them not to speak or teach any longer in the name of Christ.

What feelings of the human dimension could have lurked in John's heart during this event? Perhaps he was fearful, defensive, disappointed, remorseful, angry, stressed out, and disillusioned in those darkened conditions. Such feelings always lurk when we seek to walk with Jesus. John was no different.

Life-centered Falsehood

A third scenario establishes another way to see John's suffering in Acts 8:14-15. The good news was that Samaria had accepted the Word of God. The bad news was that a local magician was converted but had offered money to Peter and John for the power to give people the Holy Spirit by laying hands on them.

Again, Peter corrected the situation and scared the daylights out of Simon the magician. He said, "May your money perish with you, because you thought you could buy the gift of God with money! You have no part or share in this ministry, because your heart is not right before God. Repent of this wickedness and pray to the Lord. Perhaps he will forgive you for having such a thought in your heart. For I see that you are full of bitterness and captive to sin" (Acts 8:20-23).

What about the Son of Thunder? Imagine him grappling with falsehood. I have been in towns and villages where evil hung like a thick atmosphere—so dense you could almost taste it. I stopped going to one town in Kenya for this very reason. I recently felt the same way at a coffee house in Seattle, Washington. What feelings arise in such circumstances? Confusion, manipulation, abuse, and darkness, among others. Did John have such feelings in this incident in Acts 8? The Bible does not say, but John was a man like us, so it is possible he suffered the way we do.

Life-centered Sorrow

The murderous beheading of his brother, James, and the imprisonment of his best friend, Peter, undoubtedly provoked John's greatest suffering. It seems these events occurred around the year A.D. 46, thirteen years after the crucifixion of Jesus and ten years after the martyrdom of Stephen.

> It was about this time that King Herod arrested some who belonged to the church, intending to persecute them. He had James, the brother of John, put to death with the sword. When he saw that this pleased the Jews, he proceeded to seize Peter also. This happened during the Feast of Unleavened Bread. After arresting him, he put him in prison...
> —Acts 12:1-4a

In his grief and sorrow, John surely sank to the depths of darkness. Such memories of both colleagues must have drifted through his mind and many questions must have arisen. Where had he been when they were persecuted? Perhaps his absence added to his suffering. Surely there was guilt: *Why not me?* We do not know.

These probable crises for John—temptation, conflict, falsehood, and sorrow—help us connect with him for our own dream-walking difficulties. Whether in John's ancient setting or today, we ask: *How do we get through suffering to stability?*

LIFE'S STABILITY FOR *Life's* SUFFERING

As we have seen, dream-walking like Jesus requires us to seek God's divine LIFE for our human lives. That relationship is never more necessary than in suffering. The inward dwelling of God's LIFE holds the secret of stability. That is the sacred dimension of discipleship. How does it work?

It works from the inside out because God does not just show pity and concern from a distance; he shows it up close. He reveals his purpose and compassion by coming directly into our lives. He does not want to hover over us or around us; he wants to dwell in us, sharing every pain, feeling, and fear. LIFE's stability does not give us a way out of our suffering, but it does provide a way through. We may want the way out because of human dimensions, but God offers the divine dimension—the presence of his own LIFE within. Call it LIFE-in-life suffering because God dwells in us then just as much as at any other time. We just have to claim his presence.

We may think stability will come if we just know *why* something has happened. We constantly ask God, *Why?* But he remains silent because his stability relies on his answer to the question *he* wishes we would ask. That question is, *How?* How can we get through suffering to stability?

Consider God's way in terms of a thunderstorm.[40] Imagine yourself driving down a lonely road late at night with rain bombarding your windshield. Wipers frantically flip back and forth while lightning shatters the darkness. What do you do? Do you think about the circumstances that produced the storm? Do you ask, Why? No, you concentrate on watching the road, controlling the car, and looking out for others. In other words, you focus your energy on getting through the storm.

What about God at stormy times in our lives? Does he sit beside us and say, "Trust me, imitate me." Does he remind us how Jesus handled suffering? These are common thoughts, but I think differently. God says more than, "Trust me." What he says is, "Remember my presence in your life right now." He does not merely say, "Imitate me," but rather, "Invite me to participate with you."

We can only dream-walk through suffering to stability when God's LIFE dwells within our lives according to his will. Apply this to Jesus, John, and us.

> **18.** If possible, describe a time when you, or someone you know, first asked, "Why," but then learned to ask, "How."

LIFE in Christ's Suffering

Even Jesus, the first LIFE-in-life person to dream-walk the earth, asked for a way out of his final conflict before the cross. He wrestled with his own temptation to use his power outside of God's will. He prayed about the coming crucifixion every night during the last week in the Garden of Gethsemane. As it says in Hebrews, "During the days of Jesus' life on earth, he offered up prayers and petitions with loud cries and tears to the one who could save him from death, and he was heard because of his reverent submission. Although he was a son, he learned obedience from what he suffered" (Heb. 5:7-8).

Then, on that final night, intensely troubled and overwhelmed with sorrow, he broke down and prayed three times for deliverance: "He fell with his face to the ground and prayed, 'My Father, if it is possible, may this cup be taken from me. Yet not as I will, but as you will'" (Matt. 26:39). The human experience of Christ asked, "Why?" Why this way? Why not another way? Why now and not another time?

Later, while hanging on the cross, through trembling lips he asked, "My God, my God, why have you forsaken me?" (Mark 15:34). Why does evil overwhelm goodness? Why does injustice silence righteousness? Why does faith appear so weak? Why are you silent when there is such darkness and discouragement?

The Father never answered the Son's question. Instead, the Son obeyed the Father and the Father mobilized the divine response of stability through suffering by activating the LIFE that was within the incarnate Son. Jesus had prayed in the garden with that LIFE inside him. He had endured the trial with that LIFE inside him. He had been nailed to the cross while the LIFE was within him. Now he would die and be placed in a tomb, but the LIFE would still be there inside him, and he would rise on the third day by the power of that LIFE.

Human life in Jesus asked *why*, the hardest, cruelest, most bitter and despairing of all questions. Divine LIFE in Jesus provided God's answer to another question: "How?" Suffering raised the question of why; stability provided the unexpected answer to the question of how. As E. Stanley Jones said, "The cross raised the questions, Easter morning raised the Man."[41] In Christ's death, God brought the greatest good— LIFE in life—to the greatest life-minus-LIFE evil ever perpetrated on earth. Nothing has been the same since.

John's Growing Stability

Did the apostle John transcend the human dimensions of suffering and arrive at the sacred dimension of stability? Did he go on to see what was right about LIFE-in-life as he had seen it in Jesus?

We know now that he changed at the tomb, just before the ascension, and again at Pentecost. Were those the only changes in his life? No, I believe he continued changing and continued becoming a LIFE-in-life man walking the dream with Jesus. I believe he changed at each of the major events recorded in Acts. What brought him out of his temptations? The memory of LIFE within. What brought him through conflict and falsehood? LIFE within. What took him through the sorrow of his brother's execution? LIFE within.

This is in keeping with the lessons we learned from Matthew 20, where John and James wanted to be given leadership power. But Jesus offered them a cup and not a crown (20:22), a cup of suffering instead of a crown of success. Jesus asked John, "Could you endure?" Impulsively, John said, "Yes." Jesus said, "You will." How? By the power of LIFE within.

How many times did John remember this encounter? I imagine he remembered it every time he walked through suffering. Perhaps his reference to the word *light* in his inspired writings rose from those memories, so allow me to reflect on that light. Light relates to hope, while darkness relates to suffering. Each time John suffered, the LIFE within him miraculously brought LIGHT to his circumstances. Where there was LIFE, there was LIGHT. John had been a man like us, proud of his own light when only walking with Jesus. He came to realize that his most brilliant understanding of suffering was but darkness compared to God's revelation in Christ. There was only a fleeting flicker in his light, but steadfast stability in LIFE's LIGHT.

In 1 John, he reflects upon the brilliance of that divine LIGHT supplementing his dim earthly light: "God is LIGHT; in him there is no darkness at all" (1 John 1:5, emphasis added).

> That which was from the beginning, which we have heard, which we have seen with our eyes, which we have looked at and our hands have touched—this we proclaim concerning the Word of LIFE. The LIFE appeared; we have seen it and testify to it, and we proclaim to you the eternal LIFE, which was with the Father and has appeared to us.
>
> —1 John 1:1-2, emphasis added

Seven times in this passage John exclaims that they have heard, seen, looked at, and touched the LIFE of Jesus. Twice he says, "we proclaim," and once he says, "we testify." He had witnessed more than he could exclaim. He piled phrase upon phrase to explain and give urgency, yet the LIFE and the LIGHT were much more than his words could declare, far beyond his ability to write.

John changed from being a man proudly depending on his own light to one humbly depending on God's. He changed from a man explosively and impulsively forcing his light upon the suffering of others to one who realized he had been with the only One who could qualify as the LIGHT. His outlook on his own suffering was changed, and he became a dream-walking man of stability.

Now, what Jesus had said about LIGHT made sense. John's gospel begins with the bold, new declaration: "In him was LIFE, and that LIFE was the LIGHT of men" (John 1:4 emphasis added). He continues his gospel with remarkable words from Jesus: "I am the LIGHT of the world. Whoever follows me will never walk in darkness, but will have the LIGHT of LIFE" (John 8:12, emphasis added). And, "While I am in the world, I am the LIGHT of the world" (John 9:5, emphasis added).

What About Us?

As with Jesus and John, so with us. LIFE in us takes us through suffering to stability. LIFE in us "makes music out of misery, a song out of sorrow and achievement out of every accident."[42] Christ's strength did not come from without. It came from within. John's changes were produced by that LIFE within. The same is true of us. God does not pat us on the head and tell us it is going to be all right. He does not just hold our hands and say soothing words as he stands beside us. He works from the inside out.

---

19. If applicable to you, how does the book's perspective on suffering change your own viewpoint?

In our early efforts to help disciples get to stability, we concentrated on Romans 5:3-5: "Not only so, but we also rejoice in our sufferings, because we know that suffering produces perseverance; perseverance, character; and character, hope. And hope does not disappoint us, because God has poured out his love into our hearts by the Holy Spirit, whom he has given us."

We found much strength from our first perspective on that verse—but not enough. Additional strength came when the final words began to sink in that "God has poured out his love into our hearts by the Holy Spirit whom he has given us." Being stuck in

65

a previous mindset, we had interpreted it all as God outside us, somewhere off in the distance. But that is not the intent of this verse. The verse tells us he has poured out his LOVE—that is, his LIFE. Where? Into our hearts. How? Neither by a soothing ointment nor a Band-Aid, but by the Holy Spirit of LIFE, whom he has given us.

We ended those early discipleship sessions by explaining that the hope is not just for us in our own situation, but also for the next person with similar doubts, temptations, conflicts, sorrows, and false teaching. That helped a lot of people to find answers to the "Why," but it left out the "How."

The sacred dimension of discipleship provides the answer to "How." We bring hope, not just because we have suffered and persevered, not just because we have persevered and seen character change, and not because we have changed and realized hope—but because we have experienced the presence of God's LIFE in our suffering. That is the real hope we pass on to others as God saves us through suffering, and by doing so, makes suffering an instrument of his LIFE to someone else.

This second section entitled, "LIFE-fortified Foundations for the Dream-walk," now ends. We have concentrated on three essential aspects of discipleship foundations: confidence, consistency, and stability. The message has been simple: Any of these without the ingredient of God's LIFE to fortify and cement the action will end up as a walk with Jesus—but never as a walk like Jesus. And until we walk like Jesus, we will not be able to go on to the discipleship talk that results in fruitfulness, which is what we are concerned with in our next section.

PART 3

LIFE-FILLED FRUITFULNESS

As children grow, parents look forward to the time when they begin making contributions around the house. Set the table, clear the table, wash the dishes, and throw things into the trash. They feed the dog, make their beds, play with the baby, and help paint the back fence. Call it the fruitfulness of life foundations.

The third part of this book looks at the fruitfulness of LIFE-in-life foundations. This, too, takes patient time. The fruit will reflect the foundations in many ways—and nothing surpasses LIFE-filled fruitfulness.

We continue our look at the sacred dimensions of discipleship and consider three important topics: Christlikeness, evangelism, and discipling others. Just as we have looked at dream-walking possibilities for foundations, we will look again at the LIFE-in-life possibilities of fruitfulness. We will also continue to consider Jesus, John, and ourselves. Jesus provides the LIFE-in-life inspiration, John provides the LIFE-in-life transformation, and we provide the LIFE-in-life applications essential for today.

. . . .

CHAPTER 6

CHRISTLIKENESS THAT WALKS GOD'S DREAM

I DON'T LOOK much like my dad. The Irish in me won out over the German. My two sons, both of whom are adopted from a mixed union, don't look anything like me. They are good looking guys, but I'm kind of plain. Years ago, however, my wife watched my dad, my older son, and me walk across Dad's backyard. "It was so funny," she said, "you all walked the same way—same gait, body posture, and movement of shoulders." Something had been passed on from fathers to sons.

My older son now has three sons of his own. None of them look like me, either, though I have often made the facetious claim that they do. I like to show family pictures and remind people of that resemblance—except I am the one with the blue eyes. I hope that someday my wife will see us walking through a park or a mall and will note a resemblance in our walk.

Our walk with Jesus can also reveal much about our lives— our previous confidence, consistency, and stability. As we have already seen, human dimensions of that walk can overwhelm and undermine the sacred dimension of discipleship. The same can be true at the level of discipleship called Christlikeness.

THE MODERN OUTLOOK

Christlikeness makes no sense in our humanistic environment. Little in modern life-centered education and outlook advocates being like anyone let alone Jesus. This outlook pervades our society and affects us as individuals. How does it distract us from Christlikeness?

Be All You Can Be

The current perspective advocates people to be distinct, independent individuals—unlike anyone else. Much of this outlook on self-concept is established in childhood. In a matter of weeks, babies raised in the modern world learn about independence and individuality. Some say that even the game of peek-a-boo lends itself to the worldly stance.[43] Babies first learn to hide themselves by simply covering their eyes. In doing so, they learn they go on existing even when their parents cannot see them. The same is true in their view of parents, who continue existing even when their little eyes are covered. Babies reveal themselves to parents and laugh at those times when parents peek at them. Though independent of parents, they still connect to them.

Psychologists call this *attachment theory* and have spent many hours observing parents and infants playing this simple game. They have noticed several things. If parents look too intently, babies become unhappy, start to fidget, and turn away so that eye contact is broken. If babies feel watched too closely, they become uncomfortable and even cry. If parents stop looking and break eye contact, babies become alarmed and frantically cry until they get eye contact again. Or, so it has been reported.

Perhaps this baby game is only the beginning of a western socialization process that teaches independence and individuality. I remember playing the game with our first son, but I missed the game with our second because he was already six months old when he was adopted and we missed early attachment with him. My wife remembers the day when he finally let out a little sigh and melted into her arms. It took longer for him to lighten up with me. I wish we could have played peek-a-boo.

It does not stop with babyhood. As children grow up, they are raised to be independent and learn that seeking help is actually a sign of weakness. They learn to wash their own hands, clear their own plates, play by themselves, and watch TV on their own. They are sent off to schools that encourage independent thinking rather than the trust of others. "Distrust all but yourself" goes the modern directive. An American poet has said: "Trust thyself: every heart vibrates to that iron string."[44] To rely on the guidance, authority, or example of others is considered the way of a wimp.[45]

When children socialized under this philosophy become teenagers, watch out. Drama raises its horrid head, as these children demand their *freedom*. As young adults, they emerge from this educational process having learned to choose their own ways, drive their own cars, earn their own income, and get their own jobs. By the time they are older, they have learned to tackle their own problems, survive loss on their own, and face the future alone. "Flying solo is the American way," says one observer,[46] and we can add that it has become increasingly prevalent in other countries influenced by the modern ethos.

In today's societies, we choose what we want to become. We find, create, and express ourselves, taking longer these days, sometimes extending through several jobs, interests, and relationships. There is little expectation to be like anyone—unless it is a media star, a sports celebrity, or a successful personality. To be like Jesus—a loser in the view of many—hardly enters into anyone's consideration.

The modern enticement is to claim our freedom and gain our own identity. The project is called "self-identification," and it dominates popular education, religion, psychology, and even the legal world. Every person becomes his or her own project. In designing ourselves, we usually build from scratch. We choose, freely using whatever materials and circumstances in life we can to achieve our own identity.

The scheme, however, is undergoing some change. An old adage from our humanistic, life-centered roots originated from Rene Descartes who said, "I think, therefore I am." This bore the secular fruit of independence and individuality. Today, even that adage is challenged as people question rationality itself. Thinking has become suspect. One man illustrates the confusion: "I am *not* what I think I am. I am not what you think I am. I am what I think you think I am."[47] The last line has changed, however: "I am *not* what I think you think I am." Other possibilities have arisen: "I want, therefore I am"; "I am what I possess"; or "I shop, therefore I am."[48] A current version may be, "I and my I-Pod are one and the same."

An entire vocabulary has arisen around the concept of self-identification: self-interest, self-indulgence, self-development, self-enhancement, self-help, self-realization, self-knowledge, and many more.[49] We are left largely to our own imaginations as we construct these self-identities. Highly vulnerable to fashion, fads, new technology, and mass-marketed products, we frantically pursue self-construction.[50] Os Guinness has said, "The modern sense of self is chosen, not given; shifting, not stable. The modern emphasis is on *personality*, not character; on possibilities, not qualities. To be a person, therefore, has nothing to do with character and everything to do with resumes, skills, appearances, and public impressions. Such 'designer personalities' and the art of 'impression management' are vital to remaining 'hip' and 'cool.'"[51]

This one appeal of the modern world to be distinct, independent individuals cripples a biblical call to Christlikeness. It is another human dimension of life opposing the sacred dimensions of LIFE for discipleship. Christlikeness becomes meaningless to many.

Christian Entrapment

The modern outlook affects Christians. A recent study revealed that forty percent of the most active Christians in an American mega church do not tithe, twenty percent do not pray daily, and fifty percent share Christ with unbelievers less than six times a year.[52] And this was an assessment of the most active church members. Why these results?

Such outcomes could easily be attributed to our penchant for individualism. The world offers constant distractions, "a thousand modern qualifications," says one observer.[53] Tithing, prayer, and sharing Christ are not attractive possibilities when Christians pick and choose what they want to claim for their modern identity. Excessive individualism among Christians has combined with the influence of life-centered interests and the natural inclination toward independence. The important concept of the priesthood of all believers has "transmuted into the priesthood of each believer," where "everyone is entitled to his or her own opinion."[54] Private spiritualities dominate our lives,[55] and Christlikeness makes no sense in this climate of private, opinionated, excessive and spiritually schizophrenic individuality.

> **20.** On a scale of 1 to 10 with 1 being "not at all," and 10 being "completely" how would you evaluate your activity in the following: Tithing ___ Prayer ___ Bible reading ___ Evangelism ___ Reflect on your scores. In what ways could the humanistic trends of the day be influencing those scores?

Toward a Biblical Response

How do we respond to lives dictated by human interests and secular values instead of by the LIFE-centered perspective of God? Should we deny individuality and independence and turn our lives over to the professionals, lawyers, judges, and politicians?[56] Do we stop playing peek-a-boo with our children? No.

We need to consider all these issues of worldly life-centered instruction in the light of what we know about God. My own story may help. I am an American Christian and, like others, am greatly influenced by my cultural upbringing. Indirectly, that old Western adage, "I think, therefore I am" influenced me to be a very independent person. But for forty-five years, I have lived and worked in Africa, where people rely on another dictum: "We are, therefore I am."[57] Grappling with the contrasts one day in a class of 100 students at the Christian university in Nairobi, Kenya, where I taught for sixteen years, I was struck with a new realization for myself and others: "He is, therefore I am." God's existence defines our identity in special ways. How is this expressed?

Paul's declarations are well known. He said, "I have been crucified with Christ and I no longer live, but Christ lives in me" (Gal. 2:20), and "For to me, to live is Christ and to die is gain" (Phil. 1:21). In writing to the Corinthians, who were struggling with their identities, Paul said, "Do you not realize that Christ Jesus is in you?" (2 Cor. 13:5). In Colossians 2:10, Paul wrote that we are complete in Christ: "You have been given fullness in Christ, who is the head over every power and authority." Peter wrote, "His divine power has given us everything we need for life and godliness through our knowledge of him who called us by his own glory and goodness" (2 Pet. 1:3). The writer of Hebrews pointed to such identity when he referred to the way Jesus has "by one sacrifice ... made perfect forever those who are being made holy" (Heb. 10:14). Innumerable Scriptures reinforce our special identity in Christ.[58] In all, LIFE defines life in wonderful ways. No one is more interested in our individuality, freedom, and self-identity than God. We are his design and creation, needing release from life-only living and redemption for LIFE-in-life living. Jesus shows the way.

The Real Example of Jesus

"What would Jesus do?" This popular question has been around for a number of years and the commercial world has created pins, rings, bracelets, and other ornaments emblazoned with WWJD. The message behind the expression is clear: We should do whatever Jesus would have done in our circumstances.

A preferred list of Christ's ideal actions is worth emulating by the WWJD credo: Understanding God's Word, possessing a powerful prayer life, being disturbed by the Pharisees' hard-heartedness, showing compassion for people, promoting justice, performing miracles, being led by the Spirit, teaching like a master, sacrificing self, having many friendships, serving others, displaying a godly life, confronting hypocrisy, crying for those he loved, and being a faithful witness of the Father.

A list of less favored behaviors would be: He got angry, became exasperated, was often disturbed by his disciples, doubted his

Father's presence, expressed sadness, needed the support of others, wanted to be left alone, experienced severe anguish, got stressed out, claimed not to know everything, and didn't always get along with his family.[59] These behaviors remind us that at some critical points, the WWJD creed runs into trouble.

There exists, however, a deeper level of Christlikeness than mere imitation. Instead of advocating that we do only what Jesus did, it advocates that we first be what Jesus was (BWJW). Beyond a simple mimicking of Christ's actions, this sacred dimension of discipleship actually shares the LIFE behind those actions. Far beyond some religious ideal of manhood that leaves him no different than Buddha, Confucius, Mohammed, or some contemporary guru, Christ is the only LIFE-in-life Son of God providing deep roots for real Christlikeness. The *real* example of Jesus lies more deeply than just in his *ideal* behaviors.

From birth to death, the Father's LIFE was central to the Son's earthly identity. Because of that reality, Jesus did not need to imitate the Father. Imitation would have depended on observation, cleverness, pretension, and skill. It would have mimicked the Father but never been the real thing. Christ's imitation of the Father would have provided only an outward appearance. I want to suggest that a type of what I will call *infusion*, a mixture or blending of different elements in Christ's case, resulted in a perfect mixture of divine LIFE and human life. It portrayed a special kind of inward authenticity, not just an outward appearance.

Christ's earthly life was an exceptional infusion. Jesus described that sacred "infusion" to disciples who expected only human instruction. In John 14, Jesus responded to the doubts of Philip who had said, "Lord, show us the Father and that will be enough for us" (14:8). In reply, Jesus said, "Don't you believe that I am in the Father, and that the Father is in me? The words I say to you are not just my own. Rather, it is the Father, living in me, who is doing his work. Believe me when I say that I am in the Father and the Father is in me; or at least believe on the evidence of the miracles themselves" (14:10-11). Infusion!

Such thoughts had little place in Philip's mind at that time. Jesus had tried to clarify his LIFE-in-life identity to Philip and the others on many occasions:

> Do not believe me unless I do what my Father does. But if I do it, even though you do not believe me, believe the miracles, that you may know and understand that the Father is in me, and I in the Father.
>
> —John 10:37-38

> Then Jesus cried out, "When a man believes in me, he does not believe in me only, but in the one who sent me. When he looks at me, he sees the one who sent me."
>
> —John 12:44-45

Jesus always highlighted this dream-walking, LIFE-in-life reality.

Whether explaining God's Word and being a faithful witness to the Father, or getting angry and not getting along with his family, Jesus consistently lived in the same LIFE-in-life way. LIFE within him always promoted the actions we admire as well as those we choose to overlook.

This perspective on Jesus as our real example is important for us to understand. Since Jesus did not just imitate the Father, he does not ask us just to imitate him. He is our real example by reason of his identity and his LIFE-in-life existence.

Now, the question to ask is, did a disciple like John understand this message?

---

21. Satan wanted to be like God. He tempted Adam and Eve to be like God. The outcomes were rebellion and sin. Yet, the imitation of Christ is commonly encouraged today. In your own words, contrast imitation and infusion as presented in this section.

LIFE-in-life Reality

Reading through the gospels, we seldom find Jesus challenging disciples to be like him. John recorded only two such occasions at the time of the Last Supper. First, Jesus washed the feet of his disciples and said, "I have set you an example that you should do as I have done for you" (John 13:15). Later, he said, "My command is this: Love each other as I have loved you" (John 15:12). The example provided at these times was not of just one human life serving and loving another human life, but was of service and love expressed by God's LIFE in Christ. Christ's service was LIFE-in-life SERVICE; his love was LIFE-in-life LOVE. That reality, not some kind of religious idealism, was the divine challenge of the sacred dimension of discipleship.

Jesus did not call disciples to imitate his walk; he called them to the reality of the dream-walk entailing LIFE-in-life living, serving, and loving others. For this walk, Jesus promised companionship, as indicated in the Great Commission: "And surely I am with you always, to the very end of the age" (Matt. 28:20).

The dream-walk of the Lord's desire united disciples. When Jesus offered his great prayer in the gospel of John, he said,

> My prayer is not for them alone. I pray also for those who will believe in me through their message, that all of them may be one, Father, just as you are in me and I am in you. May they also be in us so that the world may believe that you have sent me. I have given them the glory that you gave me, that they may be one as we are one: I in them and you in me. May they be brought to complete unity to let the world know that you sent me and have loved them even as you have loved me.
>
> —John 17:20-23

LIFE in life creates a unique identity uniting every disciple.

Christ's real example to follow extended to his actions. He summarized his life in John 6:38 when he said, "For I have come down from heaven not to do my will but to do the will of him who sent me." His obedience to the LIFE-in-life reality of his identity prompted his actions—and he wanted nothing less for his disciples: "If you hold to my teaching, you are really my disciples. Then you will know the truth, and the truth will set you free" (John 8:31-32).

He did not say, "If you follow my example;" he said, "If you hold to my teaching." He called for obedience to the reality of LIFE-in-life—not just to words, beliefs, and religious rules. He called for submission, not just support. He aroused hope that did not just hang impossible idealistic burdens on his disciples. He went so far as to say, "I tell you the truth, if anyone keeps my word, he will never see death" (John 8:51).

The action Jesus sought in his disciples was never life-only obedience, but LIFE-in-life obedience—like his.

> If you love me, you will obey what I command....Before long, the world will not see me anymore, but you will see me. Because I live, you also will live. On that day you will realize that I am in my Father, and you are in me, and I am in you.
> —John 14:15, 19-20

When Jesus said, "I tell you the truth, anyone who has faith in me will do what I have been doing. He will do even greater things than these, because I am going to the Father" (John 14:12), what was he referring to? I believe the Lord was referring to LIFE-in-life activity. That Scripture had often puzzled me, and I never felt that my own accomplishments ever fit the category of "great," let alone "greater." But I had missed the point. Great and even greater possibilities would transpire because God's LIFE in Christ is reproduced again and again in all who believe—not by imitation, but by the same kind of infusion of LIFE into life that established Christ's own identity in the world.

The example of Jesus highlights the presence of LIFE in his life, a LIFE that prompted his every action and attitude. Christlikeness, then, takes on new significance. I believe John finally made these connections in his maturing ministry. Christlikeness was something to possess internally, not something to copy externally.

> **22.** From your own knowledge of Christ's life, choose one of his gospel activities and explain it as a LIFE-in-life activity.

Real Christlikeness for John

As we saw earlier, the Christian walk was an important part of John's ministry. He said very clearly, "Whoever claims to live in him must walk as Jesus did" (1 John 2:6). Previous religious patterns and an unenlightened walk had once confused John. But now he had been transformed three times: at Christ's resurrection, when Jesus breathed on him, and at Pentecost. John slowly understood the dream-walk of Jesus. After that, nothing else could satisfy the apostle. To "walk as Jesus did" was to dream-walk with him by LIFE-in-life transformation.

Having learned his lessons, we would expect John to advise what Jesus advised: the obedience of infused transformation and not just the tedium of mimicry. And that is exactly what he did. For John, the LIFE was real. He lavishly scattered the Word throughout his writings, giving us, for example, our well-known scriptures about LIFE:

> For God so loved the world that he gave his one and only Son, that whoever believes in him shall not perish but have eternal LIFE.
> —John 3:16 emphasis added

> Whoever believes in the Son has eternal LIFE, but whoever rejects the Son will not see LIFE, for God's wrath remains on him.
> —John 3:36

John did not say, "Whoever believes in him will have a good example to follow," but "Whoever believes in him shall not perish but have eternal LIFE." He did not say, "Whoever rejects the Son misses out on a good life," but "Whoever rejects the Son will not see LIFE."

LIFE-in-life living as seen again in his later words fascinated John:

> How great is the love the Father has lavished on us, that we should be called children of God! And that is what we are! The reason the world does not know us is that it did not know him. Dear friends, now we are children of God, and what we will be has not yet been made known. But we know that when he appears, we shall be like him, for we shall see him as he is. Everyone who has this hope in him purifies himself, just as he is pure.
> —1 John 3:1-3

We are not just adherents of a religion, but real children of the Father by reason of LIFE within. We are loved by LIFE'S LOVE, not just identified with a bunch of religious beliefs. That LOVE is passionately present in our lives, not passively promised. The world cannot grasp such infusion, and to say, "We shall be like him, for we shall see him as he is," is meaningless to the world—but the very basis of our identity. "And this is the testimony: God has given us eternal LIFE, and this LIFE is in his Son. He who has the Son has LIFE; he who does not have the Son of God does not have LIFE" (1 John 5:11-12 emphasis added).

When Jesus said, "I have come that they may have LIFE, and have it to the full" (John 10:10b, emphasis added), he declared that he came not just to give us LIFE but also to give us the qualities of that LIFE. That is, LIFE to the full. The Lord's intent can be seen in references to two qualities of life: "Peace I leave with you; my peace I give you" (John 14:27), and "I have told you this so that my joy may be in you and that your joy may be complete" (John 15:11). Jesus did not say, "Imitate my peace." What he said was, "Have my peace." Big difference. He did not say, "Imitate my joy." He said, "Have my joy." To the woman at the well, he said, "Everyone who drinks this water will be thirsty again, but whoever drinks the water I give him will never thirst. Indeed, the water I give him will become in him a spring of water welling up to eternal LIFE" (John 4:13-14 emphasis added).

John had the same outlook on the Lord's activities. He joyfully recorded the Lord's words to Nicodemus: "But whoever lives by the truth comes into the light, so that it may be seen plainly that what he has done has been done through God" (John 3:21). John understood. Doing the will of the Father required *being* the will of the Father, *being* the dream, *living* the LIFE-in-life possibilities. "Those who obey his commands live in him, and he in them. And this is how we know that he lives in us: We know it by the Spirit he gave us" (1 John 3:24).

John got it. His inspired records in the gospel and his letters reveal a man transformed by LIFE in his life. Christlikeness was something he possessed internally, not something he copied externally. He was designed for habitation, not just imitation.[60]

What about us?

---

23. We have seriously reflected on the life of John. Each of his God-inspired transformations led him to the largeness of God's dream. Write a short note, if relevant, of how John's transformations have influenced you.

THE SACRED DIMENSION OF CHRISTLIKENESS IN OUR LIVES

I set out thirty years ago to highlight Christlikeness in the life of disciples. At that time, the usual topic at this level of discipleship was called, "character." But it seemed to me that the topic was often just a list of add-ons: "Now that you're a Christian, get more love, faith, loyalty, joy, praise, and so on." My assessment prompted me to look more deeply.

A study of Philippians became my tool of choice. I was intrigued that its four chapters are filled with numerous references to good qualities of life. In fact, Paul's letter refers to about eighty different qualities needed by a Christian. The study could easily have turned into seeking such qualities in order to be a real Christian. I had, however, been greatly influenced in the 1970s by W. Ian Thomas, who contributed to a dynamic new viewpoint that became pervasive in my thinking. He said:

… It has got to become patently obvious to others that the kind of life you are living is not only highly commendable, but that it is beyond all human explanation! That it is beyond the consequences of man's capacity to imitate, and however little they may understand this, clearly the consequences only of God's capacity to reproduce himself in you. In a nutshell, this means that your fellow men must become convinced that the Lord Jesus Christ of whom you speak, is essentially Himself the ingredient of the life you live. [61]

Thomas's comments encouraged me to a search for a new kind of wholeness in Christ. As that early tool developed, four sessions from the book of Philippians pointed to Christ our life, our attitude, our aim, and our power. The single statement highlighting each session was, "Christlikeness is Christ within and to have it, we need him."[62]

I was content with that message for years, until increasingly I saw God's eternal gospel dream of his LIFE in our lives. Then, the topic of Christlikeness began to fit into God's larger plan, not just in the fourth stage of my own discipleship plan. It became more important, deeper, and not just one level among several. Christlikeness is to have God's LIFE the way Jesus had it. I kept the old tool, but found other ways to fit it into God's larger plan. As one simple example, I adapted an old bit of inspiration that said,

> In Christ we have …
> a *love* that can never be fathomed;
> a *righteousness* that can never be tarnished;
> a *peace* that can never be understood;
> a *rest* that can never be disturbed;
> a *joy* that can never be diminished;
> a *hope* that can never be disappointed;
> a *glory* that can never be clouded;
> a *light* that can never be darkened;
> a *happiness* that can never be interrupted;
> a *strength* that can never be enfeebled;
> a *purity* that can never be defiled;

a *beauty* that can never be marred;
a *wisdom* that can never be baffled; and
a *power* that can never be exhausted.
Because ...
Christ has given us his LIFE that never dies.[63]

Oswald Chambers confirmed this new perspective in one of his books: "All the qualities of a godly LIFE are characteristic of the LIFE of God; you cannot imitate the LIFE of God unless you have it"[64] (my emphasis on LIFE)

Embracing God's LIFE in our lives provides a *real* identity with options far beyond life-only living. Designed to bear the LIFE of God, we need not haphazardly fill our lives with the trivia of our world and its modern self-discovery projects.[65] With God's presence in our lives, we don't just cope with life-centered prescriptions and advice. Instead, our true identities rest on LIFE at its central place so we can respond to every situation as LIFE-in-life people. This is the Christlikeness we need. This is Christlikeness that walks God's dream. There is no other kind.

The same can be said of evangelism and the discipling of others. In the final two chapters of this book, we will see how John's experience and writing continue to inspire dream-walking possibilities for these features of discipleship mobilization.

---

24. God's kind of transformation is a radical change of perspective. John got it along the way. So have others. What about you? Is transformation of this kind happening in your life? If so, how? If not, what would happen if you allowed it?

CHAPTER 7

FROM DREAM-WALKING TO DREAM-TALKING

T HIS BOOK'S PORTRAYAL of modern trends hindering prospects for discipleship mobilization has described a worldly life-centered system that tells us to:

1. Pursue single-minded pragmatism, solitary self-reliance, and personally satisfying challenges, convictions, and pre-eminence if we want to be successfully confident
2. Seek consistency in the things that matter: expanded knowledge and technology, visual effect, spectacle, entertainment, and freedom from absolutes, authority, standards, and rigid values
3. Avoid guilt or shame about temptations, doubts, conflict, sorrow, and beliefs that interrupt health, success, and pleasure, and,
4. Demand our personal rights in the humanistic self-identification project that elevates individualism to reckless heights.

The complex web of this pervasive life-centered agenda has robbed many Christians of a biblical confidence, consistency, stability, and Christlikeness. It has also robbed evangelism, our next component of discipleship mobilization,

85

One word unites all the strands of this entangling trap of life-centeredness. That word is *knowledge*. It contrasts with the one word uniting everything about the gospel possibilities of discipleship mobilization: LIFE. Knowledge, the inhibiting word, describes the human dimensions of discipleship while LIFE, the empowering word, describes the sacred dimension.

This chapter will portray the conflict between knowledge and LIFE as a strategic battlefield for evangelistic effectiveness. Following a brief look at the conflict in our modern world, we will consider how the apostle John engaged a similar conflict after he recorded the evangelistic ways of Jesus. Then we will see our own need to consider the conflict as it affects our evangelism.

THE MODERN OUTLOOK

"Everything can be known" has become a basic assumption of our modern world.[66] Only a few experts, however, can know everything in a given field. They are the ones we admire in our knowledge-driven societies. Their popularity and power are constantly buttressed by a flood of information and constantly updated technologies. Their knowledge trumps the knowledge of average people hungering for their own meanings, but suffering from limited opportunities, dependent finances, regular crises, and many distractions.

The common person's reliance on professionals—whether in the economic, political, environmental, technological, religious, social, or legal realms—leads to dependency. Those with all the knowledge dominate those with little. Experts and those with specialized access to knowledge determine needs, identify recipients, deliver solutions, and deepen dependency. We can't do better than relying on the experts, because they know best. Right? Wrong.

Depending on experts does not always lead to positive conclusions. Today's "dazzling grasp of modern data and information often obscures a striking blind spot," which is the lack of attention to practical, down-to-earth matters of wisdom, values, responsibility, and character.[67]

Christians entangled in this modern web of knowledge seek their own alternative expertise and professionalism in the same realms of society as the secular experts. Conferences, consultations, think tanks, publications, institutions, and organizations provide experts on everything from music to missions, churches to communities, programs to power gatherings, as well as on issues from society to spirituality. The ordinary people pay, join, sit, listen, clap, stand, cheer, take notes, buy, and commit to these experts. Even so, they often lack the confidence of "knowing enough." Still hungering for meaning and significant connections, they are often drawn to today's power pastors and the social relationships of the Web.

What does all this talk of knowledge have to do with evangelism? As we have said, evangelism occurs in a battle between human knowledge and divine LIFE. John engages this battle in his gospel account.

John and the "Modernity" of His Day

The exploding knowledge that characterizes our modern world is simply the twenty-first century version of a human life-centered pursuit that began in the garden of Eden when Adam and Eve ate from the Tree of the Knowledge of Good and Evil and ignored the Tree of LIFE (Gen. 2:8-9, 3:1-6). That act created the world's first knowledge-based culture and religion. "Then the eyes of both of them were opened, and they realized they were naked; so they sewed fig leaves together and made coverings for themselves" (Gen. 3:7). This established the pattern for all future cultures and religions to be centered on the knowledge of "good and evil" as determined and shared by their own people. Modernism, or what is called modernity, was born in that garden.[68]

---

25. Read Genesis 2 and 3 in view of the battle between the pursuit of knowledge and the pursuit of LIFE. What new questions and insights, if any, come to your mind?

John's world of two thousand years ago reflected that same skewed agenda—the pursuit of knowledge—and presented him with his own battle against *modernity*. Greeks and Jews had their own experts and expectations. Closer to John's heart was the battle faced by believers. A self-proclaimed group of Christian *experts* had taken up a special position to distinguish themselves from others. They were called the "Gnostics," a label derived from the Greek word meaning *to know*, and they described themselves as Christians with superior knowledge. Like those pursuing modern knowledge, those Gnostics were on a trajectory to discover their own self-identities. Salvation, for them, was a first century form of humanistic self-realization.[69]

The concern for us is how John highlighted the gospel in such circumstances—and what that teaches us for the evangelistic component of our discipleship today. After all John's life-changing experiences and arrival at a personal knowledge of God's LIFE-in-life gospel, how did those changes and experiences translate into John's understanding of something like evangelism? What did he record on this matter, and why?

John's Gospel in a Complex Society

John wrote his gospel account about fifty years after the death of Jesus. It was the last such account written. Having been a pillar of the church in Jerusalem, John was most likely driven from Jerusalem by political and religious persecution in his late sixties. He eventually settled at Ephesus. All the rest of the New Testament had already been composed before he penned the inspired words of his gospel. Peter and Paul had died as martyrs in Rome around A.D. 67, but John may have written his gospel account in his late eighties, at least twenty years later.

Using the language and ideas of his world, but inspired by the Holy Spirit, John wrote in such a way that "Gnostics in all ages have thought that the book was written especially for them."[70] John's gospel speaks in unique ways to knowledge-driven cultures and subcultures, large and small, and to all generations and locations. At the same time, it speaks to God's sacred option—LIFE—as no other gospel does. John presented the gospel in the midst of a contest between human-centered knowledge and God-centered LIFE. Lesslie Newbigin summarizes the book of John by saying,

> The first twelve chapters trace with relentless and cumulative power the total inability of even the best and most godly to grasp what is being offered; and they end with the absolute rejection of Jesus ... And then, from Chapter 13 to 17 we find ourselves in an entirely different world, a world in which Jesus himself is the radiating center of light and love (illuminating) all circumstances and future history... On the one side, Jesus is the one who subverts true religion and contradicts ordinary rationality; on the other, he is the center and the source of all truth.[71]

"In the beginning" are the first words of John's gospel. They immediately take us back to the same words at the opening of the book of Genesis, where the gospel battle began between the choice of the Tree of the Knowledge of Good and Evil or the Tree of LIFE. The choice for Adam and Eve was whether to live God's way or their own ways. The battle, as seen by John in his day, centered upon the same conflict.

> In the beginning was the Word, and the Word was with God, and the Word was God. He was with God in the beginning. Through him all things were made; without him nothing was made that has been made. In him was LIFE, and that LIFE was the LIGHT of men. The LIGHT shines in the darkness, but the darkness has not understood it."
>
> —John 1:1-5, emphasis added

In his knowledge-driven world immersed in words about life, John introduced his gospel with the WORD who is the LIFE. To the religious arguments of the Greeks, Romans, and Jews, John presented God's eternal dream of LIFE-centered living that had no place in their life-centered thinking. Though the various versions of that knowledge-driven world of the first century had a place for either God or the gods, John presented God as One far beyond their religious categories and classifications. He was "I AM" instead of "He is." He was the subject of real LIFE, not an object in the improvised life of selected knowledge systems. Instead of their place for God in their dreams, he presented God's place for them in his dream. John's beginning points toward the goal of his writing as he goes on to reveal special gospel events in the time of Christ on earth.

John the Baptist, Andrew, Philip, the Samaritan woman, the blind man, Lazarus, and the apostle himself brought others to Christ according to John's gospel.[72] The book is itself a bold and brilliant declaration of the gospel to Jew and non-Jew alike. In these and other ways, it sets out the eternal battle between the plans of life-centered knowledge and the LIFE-centered plan of God. For John, however, Jesus himself best revealed the nature of evangelism on such a battlefield.

> **26.** From the brief descriptions that follow, list two to three ways John presented the gospel into the conflict we are considering.

CHRIST'S OWN EVANGELISM

John records three instances of Christ's evangelistic efforts. The first is when Jesus appealed to a professional in the religious knowledge system of the day (John 3). In the second, Jesus appealed to an impoverished woman at the mercy of that system (John 4). And in the third, he spoke to a mixed synagogue crowd of both professionals and common people (John 6). In all three instances, Jesus focused on God's gospel dream of LIFE in life—and we see how this Holy Dream-walker was a Dream-talker.

Nicodemus, the Professionally Religious (John 3)

In the third chapter of John, the apostle calls attention to Christ's evangelistic ways with a Pharisee named Nicodemus (3:1).

He was a member of the Jewish ruling council who had come to Jesus secretly at night.

Nicodemus began the discussion with safe, religious issues pertaining to life (teaching and miracles). Jesus listened, but he got right past religion to the main issue, the need of LIFE for ultimate destiny: "I tell you the truth, no one can see the kingdom of God unless he is born again" (3:3).

The soul-searching Pharisee tried to grasp Christ's reply from his own life-centered perspective by asking, "How can a man be born when he is old? ... Surely he cannot enter a second time into his mother's womb to be born!"(3:4). Again Jesus brought him right back to the main issue—LIFE: "I tell you the truth, no one can enter the kingdom of God unless he is born of water and the Spirit. Flesh gives birth to flesh, but the Spirit gives birth to spirit. You should not be surprised at my saying, 'You must be born again'" (3:5-7). "How can this be?" Nicodemus asked (John 3:9). The Pharisee was thinking of earthly processes of knowledge, but Jesus boldly declared the new heavenly origins of LIFE. He asked Nicodemus, "I have spoken to you of earthly things and you do not believe; how then will you believe if I speak of heavenly things?" (3:12).

The man had to be shocked out of the life-centered perspective he had been taught and for which he was an instructor. This *professional* thinker had to accept completely new ways of reasoning. The proficient speaker had to become speechless. This man who knew everything had to come to the place where he recognized he knew nothing. A new origin required a new beginning. A new beginning required a new authority. A new authority required a new trust. And a new trust required a new LIFE-in-life change of everything. The man was stunned.

Jesus kept to the main issue and gave us one of the Bible's beloved verses, John 3:16: "For God so loved the world that he gave his one and only Son, that whoever believes in him shall not perish but have eternal LIFE." In this single statement, the Son showed that LIFE illuminates the meaning of God's LOVE, the meaning of the Father-Son relationship, the meaning of "whoever believes," and the meaning of eternal LIFE.

Jesus continued to make L$_{\text{IFE}}$ the main issue, linking it to salvation, forgiveness, and death: "For God did not send his Son into the world to condemn the world, but to save the world through him. Whoever believes in him is not condemned, but whoever does not believe stands condemned already because he has not believed in the name of God's one and only Son" (3: 17-18).

Jesus then personalized his appeal. He adopted the most obvious context that he and Nicodemus shared—the darkness around them, which was chosen by Nicodemus as he had come to Jesus "at night."

> This is the verdict: Light has come into the world, but men loved darkness instead of light because their deeds were evil. Everyone who does evil hates the light, and will not come into the light for fear that his deeds will be exposed. But whoever lives by the truth comes into the light, so that it may be seen plainly that what he has done has been done through God.
>
> —John 3:19-21

The *enlightened* professional needed light. His own rational illumination was but the darkness of life alone; Nicodemus needed the light of L$_{\text{IFE}}$. "In him was life, and that life was the light of men" (John 1:4). If Nicodemus were a true soul-searcher, he would not be satisfied until he walked out of his darkness and into God's light.

The Samaritan Woman, the Passively Religious (John 4)

John's clever, Spirit-inspired contrast to Nicodemus is the abused woman of John 4. She was dependent on what she had heard from the professionals of her day. We know the story. Jesus had to travel through Samaria to get to Galilee, an unpleasant journey because of the animosity between Jews and Samaritans. At Sychar, he stopped at Jacob's well while his disciples went into the market.

A Samaritan woman came to draw water, and Jesus asked for a drink. This request led to a second opportunity to bring the message of L$_{\text{IFE}}$ to another life. The woman passively responded with an answer the professionals of her day had told her: "Jews do not associate with Samaritans" (4:9). Jesus, in dream-walking passion, answered her, "If you knew the gift of God and who it is that asks you for a drink, you would have asked him and he would have given you living water" (4:10).

As with Nicodemus, Jesus got right to the point—LIFE. She heard only *life*, however, and relied on her life-centered thinking—no pot was around for collecting water. She went on to refer again to what the religious professionals of her day had told her: "Are you greater than our father Jacob, who gave us the well and drank from it himself, as did also his sons and his flocks and herds?" (4:12). Jesus, for his part, could not stay off the dream-walking message: "Everyone who drinks this water will be thirsty again, but whoever drinks the water I give him will never thirst. Indeed, the water I give him will become in him a spring of water welling up to eternal LIFE" (4:13-14 emphasis added).

Just as Jesus could not get off his LIFE-in-life message, the woman could not get off her life-only understanding, and she asked for the Lord's water so she wouldn't have to come to the well anymore (4:15). At this point, Jesus got personal and asked her to call her husband and come back with him. As we know, she replied by saying she had no husband. When the Lord revealed his own knowledge of her, the woman recognized that she was talking to "a prophet." But she went right back to a dependent perspective by contrasting Samaritan worship on the mountain and Jewish worship in Jerusalem (4:19-20).

Jesus continued to speak from a LIFE-in-life perspective. The day was coming, he told her, when worship would not be determined by life, whether Samaritan or Jewish, but by LIFE: "Yet a time is coming and has now come when the true worshipers will worship the Father in spirit and truth, for they are the kind of worshipers the Father seeks. God is spirit, and his worshipers must worship in spirit and in truth" (4:23-24).

She then remembered one more thing she had learned from the professionals: "I know that Messiah (called Christ) is coming. When he comes, he will explain everything to us" (4:25). Jesus simply said, "I who speak to you am he" (4:26). No argument, no superior knowledge, just the facts. The Word replaced religious words; real LIFE replaced religious knowledge. The woman believed and ran back to Sychar to tell the people, and "many of the Samaritans from that town believed in him because of the woman's testimony" (4:39).

Evangelism at a Synagogue in Capernaum (John 6)

One more incident allowed John to illustrate how Christ emphasized LIFE in dream-talking evangelism. Unlike the previous events where Jesus spoke to one person, here he spoke to a great crowd of Jews (6:30-69). Some of these were the religious professionals of the day, and others were the common folk who depended on them.

The professionals dominated the dialogue. They asserted authority by demanding a miracle and reminding Christ, and the crowd, of their knowledge of Moses in the wilderness providing bread from heaven. They asked Jesus to provide a miraculous sign so they could see it and believe in him (6:30-31). The Lord responded by requiring them to see beyond life to LIFE, beyond Moses to God himself, beyond bread that decayed to bread that is eternal. Jesus told them, "It is not Moses who has given you the bread from heaven, but it is my Father who gives you the true bread from heaven. For the bread of God is he who comes down from heaven and gives life to the world" (6:32-33). Listeners in the crowd scoffed and said, "Sir ... from now on give us this bread" (6:34).

The Lord's bold reply cut right to the issue of LIFE: "I am the bread of LIFE. He who comes to me will never go hungry, and he who believes in me will never be thirsty" (6:35 emphasis added). The reply left the crowd grumbling. For one thing, what did Jesus mean when he said, "I have come down from heaven not to do my will but to do the will of him who sent me" (6:38)? They asked each other, "Is this not Jesus, the son of Joseph, whose father and mother we know? How can he now say, 'I came down from heaven'?" (6:42). Another problem was that he did the unthinkable and called God "Father."

For my Father's will is that everyone who looks to the Son and believes in him shall have eternal life, and I will raise him up at the last day.

—6:40 emphasis added

Their life-minus-LIFE thinking excluded any possibility of a Father-Son relationship describing God. They judged everything by their knowledge of life because they did not know LIFE. The Jewish leaders grumbled and again asserted superior knowledge, reminding everyone that Jesus was only the son of Joseph.

Jesus replied, and now his words touched on that very subject of knowledge, which was the major conflict of the day. He reminded them that their own prophets had said that God himself would teach his people—and the audience could not miss the fact of his own teaching at that very moment. True knowledge originates in LIFE. Then he said, "Everyone who listens to the Father and learns from him comes to me" (6:45). Then, back to the subject of LIFE, for "he who believes has everlasting LIFE" (6:47 emphasis added).

By comparing the manna in the wilderness, that extended life only for a while, to himself, Jesus declared that he was the bread a person could eat and never die (6:48-50). He clarified the issue precisely: "I am the living bread that came down from heaven. If anyone eats of this bread, he will live forever. This bread is my flesh, which I will give for the life of the world" (6:51).

As he had done with Nicodemus and the Samaritan woman, Jesus shocked them with that last statement, touching raw nerves. The religious experts began to argue among themselves (6:52). Jesus, however, would not let the moment decline to a life-centered argument, so he gave them another jolt:

I tell you the truth, unless you eat the flesh of the Son of Man and drink his blood, you have no LIFE in you. Whoever eats my flesh and drinks my blood has eternal life, and I will raise him up at the last day. For my flesh is real food and my blood is real drink. Whoever eats my flesh and drinks my blood remains in me, and I in him. Just as the living Father sent me and I live

95

because of the Father, so the one who feeds on me will live because of me.

—6:53-57 emphasis added

On hearing this, the disciples themselves grumbled, and Jesus went on to speak to them about the reality of his LIFE intimately connected to the Father, making one of his most crucial statements to them: "The Spirit gives LIFE; the flesh counts for nothing. The words I have spoken to you are spirit and they are LIFE" (6:63, emphasis added).

> **27.** If you can, highlight one memorable statement from each of the three events in John 3,4 and 6. Write the statements in your journal and tell why you chose them.

LIFE is everything; life by itself is nothing.

It was too much for these religious people. Many of his own disciples deserted him that day (6:66). Turning to the Twelve, he gave them the opportunity to retreat as well. But Peter spoke up for the disciples: "Lord, to whom shall we go? You have the words of eternal life. We believe and know that you are the Holy One of God" (6:68-69). Peter hardly knew what he was talking about.

Chapters three, four, and six of John's gospel set out a clear testimony of Christ's evangelism. John's inspired intent is obvious: Jesus was not only a dream-walker, he was also a dream-talker. LIFE was central to his methods and his message. Nicodemus, the Samaritan woman, and the people at the synagogue in Capernaum were all drawn to their knowledge of life—birth, water, and bread. But in each case, Jesus brought them to eternal LIFE—new life, living water, and endless provision. Notice six aspects of his gospel communication:

- he listened first
- he heard their misguided dependence on a knowledge related to life

- he made statements that led them to face LIFE's perspective on the issues
- he never got sidetracked from the subject of LIFE
- he shocked them with his replies to their own perspectives, and
- he personalized the final encounter.

How can we offer the same gift of LIFE in our evangelism for discipleship mobilization?

BECOMING DREAM-TALKERS

When today's evangelism becomes trapped in arguments about knowledge, it shows that it has lost sight of the glory and the power of LIFE. With an emphasis on knowledge, we show that, like Adam, Eve, and the Gnostics of John's day, we are more attracted to the Tree of the Knowledge of Good and Evil than the Tree of LIFE. Ensnared by knowledge, we turn evangelism into a defense of our lives, viewpoints, religions, churches, and our plans—missing the freedom of LIFE that focuses on God at the center, the wonder of his revelation, the frankness of faith, and the completeness of God's plan outlasting all plans. We are too easily caught up in the vast modern system of exploding knowledge. How can we put LIFE first in our gospel-sharing the way Jesus did? Three observations are important.

Be Alert to the Battle

Jesus was keenly alert to the primal battle between the plans of life-centered knowledge and the LIFE-centered plan of God that began in the Garden of Eden. Perhaps the absence of this sharp awareness among today's Christians explains why it takes 1000 Christians and six of their pastors to win one person to Christ per year in the United States.[73] A radio speaker in 2008 reported how one convert cost American churches $320,000—probably because outreach was not a priority and in-house activities were. Perhaps blindness to a battle explains why 97 percent of the church has no involvement in any sort of evangelism according to another observer who also reported that only one percent of its church leadership readers had witnessed to someone recently, the rest were lukewarm or cold.[74]

If we are going to be more effective in evangelism today, we will have to take seriously the battle between the Tree of Knowledge of Good and Evil and the Tree of LIFE.

> **28.** Think back on your involvement, or lack of involvement, in evangelism. In what way, if any, has your situation centered around religious knowledge more than LIFE?

Keep LIFE Our Main Concern

The battle was just the context of evangelism for Jesus, however, and that is how we must know it. Informed of its subtleties, influence, and pundits, we must, like Jesus, keep as our main concern the LIFE that forgives, saves, redeems, and makes all things new. The source and nature of that LIFE is the true means of evangelism beyond message and method. Jesus emphasized this in John 15:1-8:

> I am the true vine, and my Father is the gardener. He cuts off every branch in me that bears no fruit, while every branch that does bear fruit he prunes so that it will be even more fruitful. You are already clean because of the word I have spoken to you. Remain in me, and I will remain in you. No branch can bear fruit by itself; it must remain in the vine. Neither can you bear fruit unless you remain in me. I am the vine; you are the branches. If a man remains in me and I in him, he will bear much fruit; apart from me you can do nothing. If anyone does not remain in me, he is like a branch that is thrown away and withers; such branches are picked up, thrown into the fire and burned. If you remain in me and my words remain in you, ask whatever you wish, and it will be given you. This is to my Father's glory, that you bear much fruit, showing yourselves to be my disciples.

More than providing a gospel message and a gospel method, Jesus provides the gospel means of evangelism. He is the source of LIFE, the one from whom the lost find LIFE, the one who forgives the sinner by the standards of LIFE, the one who leads the unbeliever to surrender to LIFE, and the one who teaches the born-again to live by LIFE. Gospel message and methods are dependent on gospel means.

Share LIFE

Evangelism is more than just sharing your testimony, a message, or Bible verses. As John 15 shows, God's LIFE is given to be shared. Jesus expects disciples to be the gospel means to others in a secondary sense, as a branch to the vine. Jesus is the primary source; we are the secondary. Just as we may not understand how a fruitful plant's sap flows from the roots, through the vine, and into branches that leaf, bud, bloom, and yield fruit, neither do we understand the exact process by which God's LIFE flows from the Father into Jesus Christ, on to his disciples—and miraculously through the lives of those disciples on to others. But it does.

The Lord's metaphor about his being the true vine and the Father being the gardener came from the vineyards of his day. A more apt metaphor for today may be industrial. Large power-generating plants transmit electricity to our homes and offices. Cables carry more power than we dare try managing ourselves. But eventually, that electricity comes down to a small wire, which, linked to a receptor, produces light. God the Father is like the power source; God the Son is like the cable; and God the Holy Spirit is like the small wire connected to every believer—the receptors which project the light. Disconnected from the source, we become useless in evangelism. Light bulbs with no glow, having broken filaments instead. But as we remain connected, LIFE flows into our lives to flow out again into the lives of others.

To summarize, we can become more effective dream-talkers in our evangelism when we keep alert to the battle, make LIFE the main concern, and share LIFE with others.

> **29.** Describe the relationship between dream-walking and dream-talking as you see it? How does it apply to you?

When we are alert, focused, and eager to share like Jesus, we will be better listeners, more skillful talkers, and more personally engaging. Our dream-walking will become dream-talking, a new level of evangelistic outreach that will go on to make the follow-up and final component of our study—discipleship—absolutely necessary for effective mobilization.

CHAPTER 8

DREAM-WALKING
DISCIPLESHIP

LIKE WATCHING A house burn, a car smashed, or a plan fall apart, I watched with dismay as my original design for discipleship went off in the wrong direction. It had become passively focused on certain levels of shared knowledge, rather than powerfully formed on a higher level by the shared LIFE of God within those discipled. The presence of LIFE, the sacred dimension of discipleship, had always been my intention. But the intended relationship was often replaced by the exercise of getting someone to purchase some books, fill in the blanks, and complete the sentences.

Looking back on those efforts, I now recognize that I had not been passionate or persistent enough about that shared LIFE. The burden for that message, method, and means of evangelism and discipleship grew belatedly along the way. The fleshly patterns of others also entered into the equation. For example, an old communication game applied: Start a message at one end of a line of twelve people, whisper it in the ear of the first person, and have it whispered down the line, only to hear the final message from the last person as a completely garbled version.

The message of God's LIFE in human lives became skewed when related knowledge about that LIFE was distorted. Languages

101

proved to be a big handicap when existing vocabularies had few if any ways to distinguish between God's LIFE and human life, not to mention the life of plants, animals, and insects.[75] In English, writing was not a problem because we could distinguish them visually: LIFE and life. But even in English, speaking the difference was difficult. More reference to *God's* LIFE and *human life* helped. Many speakers referred to *big* LIFE and *small life*. That spoke to the informed, but not to the average listener. Unfortunately, some speakers also turned *big* LIFE into *bigger life*, a common tendency toward life-centered thinking and desires, rather than LIFE-centered thought and desire.

It is possible to understand the sacred dimensions of discipleship and yet find it a challenge to communicate it in a Christian's *religious* world that is quite satisfied with long-established patterns of church, theology, thought, attitude, and behavior. As we have seen, John faced this same kind of challenge.

A FINAL LOOK AT JOHN'S DREAM-WALK

It is difficult to trace John's dream-walk with Jesus after John was forced out of Jerusalem where he, along with Peter, James, and others, had focused on ministry to Christians with a Jewish heritage. Trying to put the finishing brushstrokes on our portrait of John, I will have to rely on what church history tells us, so I will propose a scenario.

A Scenario of John's Later Life

It seems that John was shipwrecked near Ephesus as he fled from Jerusalem around A.D. 70. He apparently arrived in time to check the spread of heresies that were springing up after Paul's death in A.D. 67. Perhaps the elders and leaders of that church had failed to follow Paul's advice (Acts 19:1-20:1; 20:17-38). In any event, Paul's words to them at his farewell were prophetic:

> Keep watch over yourselves and all the flock of which the Holy Spirit has made you overseers. Be shepherds of the church of

God, which he bought with his own blood. I know that after I leave, savage wolves will come in among you and will not spare the flock. Even from your own number men will arise and distort the truth in order to draw away disciples after them. So be on your guard!

—Acts 20:28-31a

Perhaps the condition of the church prompted the Holy Spirit to cause John to leave Jerusalem and the Jews, go to the more secular city of Ephesus, and write his gospel account. Perhaps Life was already missing from the Christian experience of Paul's converts at Ephesus, offering "savage wolves" and false teachers the opportunity to ravage the flock with distorted truth.

From the time he was in his late sixties, Ephesus became John's new ministry base. Most likely he became concerned about the seven churches of Asia Minor —Ephesus, Smyrna, Pergamum, Thyatira, Sardis, Philadelphia, and Laodicea—as described in his inspired account of the book of Revelation (Rev. 1:11). While at Ephesus, he was apparently arrested and taken to Rome. When he eluded death in that center of empire, he was sent in exile to Patmos, where he wrote the book of Revelation (Rev. 1:9). With a later change of Rome's emperors, John was released from the island in his late eighties and returned to Ephesus until his death at the end of the century or beyond.

In his ministry, John constantly encountered people who denied Life's truth and instead fostered their own knowledge and interpretations of that truth (1 John 4:1; 2 John 7). Claiming special knowledge, they disputed John's authority and ability (3 John 9-10).

What did John do with lasting effect? He made disciples. It is possible that he started this task with Ignatius of Antioch when he was still in Jerusalem. This disciple eventually became a martyr fifteen to twenty years after John's own death, and Ignatius often referred to John's gospel in his own discipleship tools and books.

John most likely continued his discipleship mobilization from his earliest times in Ephesus. One famous man who was said to have come under that ministry was Polycarp of Smyrna, an early church father. Polycarp went on to disciple Irenaeus, who began to travel everywhere so that, by the end of the second century, the fourth gospel was well known throughout Africa, Asia Minor, Italy, Gaul, and Syria.[76] All these men wrote what we would now call discipleship tools and books for the early church, and their writings often referred to "the old man at Ephesus."[77]

There is considerable evidence that John sought a discipleship that resulted in a strategic fellowship of like-minded men and women. His three epistles point further to this aim. In 1 John 1:5-7, he wrote to his "children":

> This is the message we have heard from him and declare to you: God is light; in him there is no darkness at all. If we claim to have fellowship with him yet walk in the darkness, we lie and do not live by the truth. But if we walk in the light, as he is in the light, we have fellowship with one another, and the blood of Jesus, his Son, purifies us from all sin.

To "the chosen woman and her children," he wrote in 2 John 1:4, "It has given me great joy to find some of your children walking in the truth, just as the Father commanded us." To his "dear friend" Gaius, an elder, he wrote in 3 John 1:3-4, "It gave me great joy to have some brothers come and tell about your faithfulness to the truth and how you continue to walk in the truth. I have no greater joy than to hear that my children are walking in the truth."

When John wrote about his children, I believe he had LIFE-in-life people in mind. His children were God's children by reason of shared LIFE. His discipleship was about passing on LIFE, not just religious knowledge. I cannot read his gospel and trace his dream-walk and avoid that conclusion. His discipleship and his fellowship were based on that LIFE. He aimed at that kind of unity, powerfully prompted, I believe, by Christ's prayer of John 17.

John 17 – Beginning at a Prayer

John is the only gospel writer who recorded the world-embracing discipleship prayer of Jesus. Like others, the apostle had received the Great Commission as recorded by Matthew (28:18-20). But John was perhaps the only one deeply moved by Jesus praying for himself, his disciples, and for all believers.

Knowing what we now know about John, it seems that the prayer of John 17 may have become John's primary basis for the discipleship mobilization so central to his life. I believe this prayer was not just printed by John's hand but was imprinted on his heart. I don't think he finished the inspired task and said, "Nice prayer." I think it much more likely that John finished writing these words and said something like, "This will become the fire of my ministry."

What would a ministry set on fire by this prayer look like for John? It would ...

- Be set on fire by LIFE's brilliant glory as seen in the Son and the Father. Like a mirror catching the rays of the sun and aiming them at a small pile of kindling, this brilliant glory started a fire in John's heart. The opposite? No LIFE, no heavenly glory. As Jesus said, "Father, the time has come. Glorify your Son, that your Son may glorify you" (John 17:1).

- Begin from the spark of LIFE given from God himself, from the fire that is never extinguished—eternal life. Only an intimate knowledge of God's ultimate LIFE measures up to the discipleship task. The opposite? No LIFE, no fire. No intimate knowledge of LIFE, no heat— just smoke. "Father, the time has come. Glorify your Son, that your Son may glorify you. For you granted him authority over all people that he might give eternal life to all those you have given him. Now this is eternal life: that they may know you, the only true God, and Jesus Christ, whom you have sent" (John 17:1-3).

- Require earthly labor that culminates in heaven's presence before the Father, just like Jesus: "I have brought you glory on earth by completing the work you gave me to do. And now, Father, glorify me in your presence with the glory I had with you before the world began" (John 17:4-5). The opposite? No LIFE-centered labor, no reward.

- Become a fire spreading on to the lives of disciples who obey, understand deeply, accept the Word, live with bold certainty, and value the Lord's discipleship prayer for themselves. The opposite? No LIFE and no LIFE qualities in the labor. "I have revealed you to those whom you gave me out of the world. They were yours; you gave them to me and they have obeyed your word. Now they know that everything you have given me comes from you. For I gave them the words you gave me and they accepted them. They knew with certainty that I came from you, and they believed that you sent me. I pray for them. I am not praying for the world, but for those you have given me, for they are yours" (John 17:6-9).

- Be an all-consuming fire in all of life for John, as it was for Jesus. As Jesus said, "All I have is yours, and all you have is mine. And glory has come to me through them" (John 17:10). This means all of life because the Father had promised all of LIFE. The results would only be seen beyond his life. The opposite? No LIFE—just the fleeting fires of life.

- Require a divine unity initiated by LIFE in his life and in the lives of his disciples, a unity that could not be destroyed by distance or the human dimensions of life. As Jesus said, "I will remain in the world no longer, but they are still in the world, and I am coming to you. Holy Father, protect them by the power of your name—the name you gave me—so that they may be one as we are one" (John 17:11). The opposite? No LIFE, no unity.

- Require the Lord's own protection. As Jesus said, "While I was with them, I protected them and kept them safe by that name you gave me. None has been lost except the one doomed to destruction so that Scripture would be fulfilled" (John 17:12). With LIFE, disciples would continue to experience the promised presence of the Lord, who said "Surely I am with you always, to the very end of the age" (Matt. 28:20). The opposite? No LIFE, no discipleship defense.

- Be an exultant task rising from LIFE's joy within. Jesus sought the full measure of his own joy for John and others: "I am coming to you now, but I say these things while I am still in the world, so that they may have the full measure of my joy within them" (John 17:13). The opposite? No LIFE, no joy in the work.
- Be a fire many would try to extinguish through opposition, hostility, distractions, and combative alternatives. Jesus knew the dangers: "I have given them your word and the world has hated them, for they are not of the world any more than I am of the world. My prayer is not that you take them out of the world but that you protect them from the evil one. They are not of the world, even as I am not of it" (John 17:14-16). The opposite? No LIFE, no ability to keep burning.
- Be a holy fire, sanctified by truth. God's Word would be ever available, ever at work, because Jesus said, "Sanctify them by the truth; your word is truth. As you sent me into the world, I have sent them into the world. For them I sanctify myself, that they too may be truly sanctified" (John 17:17-19). The opposite? No LIFE, no truth.
- Be a spreading fire fueled by shared LIFE. God's LIFE would always lead to growth and expansion—from Jerusalem, Judea, Samaria, and the uttermost parts of the world. Jesus had prayed, "My prayer is not for them alone. I pray also for those who will believe in me through their message, that all of them may be one, Father, just as you are in me and I am in you. May they also be in us so that the world may believe that you have sent me" (John 17:20-21). The opposite? No LIFE, no LIFE-centered mobilization and increase.
- Yield the glory and unity of LIFE, not the individual fame and disunity of life. A profound glory would be available. A complete unity would be possible. "I have given them the glory that you gave me, that they may be one as we are one: I in them and you in me. May they be brought to complete unity to let the world know that you sent me and have loved them even as you have loved me. Father, I want

those you have given me to be with me where I am, and to see my glory, the glory you have given me because you loved me before the creation of the world" (John 17:22-24). The opposite? No LIFE, no divine results.

- Be a nonstop, unbroken, continuous fire. Why? Because Jesus would continue to make God known in all his power: "Righteous Father, though the world does not know you, I know you, and they know that you have sent me. I have made you known to them, and will continue to make you known in order that the love you have for me may be in them and that I myself may be in them" (John 17:25-26). The opposite? No LIFE, no permanence.

These thirteen dynamics of discipleship mobilization can be extracted from the Lord's discipleship prayer in John 17. Each of them has a LIFE-in-life basis, and each implies the extreme danger of discipleship without LIFE. Every time Jesus used the word *one* to describe a unique unity (verses 11, 20, 22, 23, and 26), he was declaring God's gospel intent as the basis of discipleship mobilization. Don't miss this, says Eugene Peterson: "Father, Son and every last one of us by the prayer and the cross of Jesus and the work of the Holy Spirit are made one."[78]

The opposites of the thirteen dynamics listed above explain a great deal about the frequent status of many ineffective Christians, churches, and Christian communities.

> **30.** The opposites of a ministry set on fire by Christ's prayer are listed in the thirteen dynamics. All begin with "No LIFE . . . ." Of the thirteen deficiencies we must avoid, which one is of particular interest to you? Why?

I believe the positive dynamics surging from the Lord's discipleship prayer of John 17 started a fire for John's discipleship. Picture him writing the fourth gospel, the book of Revelation, and his three epistles with this sacred fire passionately burning in his life. Picture yourself fired up in this way and mobilizing others.

> **31.** For your journal, write how at least three of these thirteen dynamics have appealed to you as you have read them. To what extent do you want Christ's prayer to be the source of your own involvement in discipleship mobilization?

I hope you have learned as much from John, his writings, and his experiences as I have. Looking back on my initial discipleship mobilization, I wish I had believed then what I believe now. As with John, God has been patient with me—really patient. I am glad I started, however. I would have missed certain lessons without that beginning. Perhaps you are at that beginning point. I hope so. In these concluding pages, I want to help you make a start.

FINDING OTHERS TO DREAM-WALK WITH US

If you have kept a journal while reading this book—even a partial and brief journal, whether on paper or electronically—you will be better prepared to begin a discipleship journey with someone else. This book was designed to become a tool for discipleship mobilization and multiplication. I want you to be able to look back at this book and your journal and identify life-changing moments prompted by a new understanding of God's eternal dream to bring his LIFE into your life and the lives of people around you.

Our thirty-year mobilization effort has been based on a social pattern in which everyone, you and me included, has participated. That pattern is the fact that *we all have a social network.* Some say that each person's network consists of as many as 120 people whom we know closely and intimately, such as family members, friends, schoolmates, colleagues at work, fellow members at clubs, neighbors, church members, and people in other social settings.

We have simply encouraged new disciplers to disciple such people. None of us will succeed in discipling all 120 prospects, but we could feasibly disciple ten percent of them—twelve. Of those twelve, we have learned from experience that only two or three will go on to disciple their social networks. Like us, they will probably find only twelve who may be responsive. Yet, disciples discipling disciples is the way to see mobilization and multiplication.

Notice that one's social network is not confined to church members. Whenever we limit our discipling possibilities to our own church walls, we cripple the Lord's intent to reach the world. We cannot reach the world by stopping at our walls.

> **32.** Try to list twelve people in your social network whom you could consider reaching for dream-walking purposes. It is best for men to reach men and women to reach women, unless there are direct family connections to you.

Therefore, my hope has been that you would finish this book and say, "No. I'm not finished. I'm just beginning. I need to share this with someone else." If this has been your conviction, I want to lay out a simple way to use this book to disciple others. The question now is, How can you begin? I will suggest four initial steps.

Begin with the End in Mind

Envision what God can do in the lives of others when they get caught in the passion of his gospel dream for their lives. Envision the results of your discipleship efforts for the next ten years. When I begin a discipling relationship, I begin with the hope that the two of us will, in ten years, become 512—by simply finding one new person per year to disciple and send on to disciple others who do the same. This strategy comes from the apostle Paul: "And the things you have heard me say in the presence of many witnesses entrust to reliable men who will also be qualified to teach others" (2 Tim. 2:2).

Set yearly goals for yourself. Find those who will join you in your availability to God. Follow up on such people no matter where they go. Keep God's dream before them always. Be part of that dream.

Be What You Challenge Others to Be

Live the dream as Jesus did. Walk it with him. Talk it like him. Perfectly? No, you will never be perfect, but you can always be growing and maturing. Walk as though you are carrying $10,000 in your pocket, not just ten cents. Move like you are dream-walking, not just walking. Talk like you are dream-talking, not just talking. Let your thoughts, attitudes, and behaviors reflect God's dream for your life.

You may want to read or reread *God's Dream: A Refreshing Look at the Gospel,* my first book preceding this one. You may want to revisit your journal and respond to more of the exercises than you did originally. You may need to take some time off to pray, read the Word, and seek God's guidance. You may need to spend time seeking advice from a loved one, friend, or colleague. Whatever you do, do not try starting a fire. Find the God-intended, LIFE-centered fire within you.

Choose Others Carefully

I suggest that you encourage a prospective disciple to read *God's Dream.* You could meet together periodically to discuss its contents. Those shared times could give you a measure of a potential disciple's enthusiasm for LIFE-in-life living, and that would help you determine whether that person is ready to be discipled.

At the right time, get your disciple started with *Dream-walking: The Sacred Dimensions of Discipleship* and a personal journal. The relationship could require two months of meetings while new disciples digest the contents and journal their experiences. Be sure to choose someone who can stay the course and really catch the fire. That does not mean you ignore others, but it does mean you reserve discipleship for the few.

111

Keep your first step in mind—see the end from the beginning. Seek people who show the most likelihood of going on to disciple others. As one disciple-maker said, "Weak links in the chain do break the reproductive process. Every time you lose a link you cut your ultimate production in half."[79] Jim Collins has said, "The old adage 'People are our most important asset' is wrong. People are not your most important asset. The right people are."[80] He went on to say that the choice of right people has more to do with character and attitude than with knowledge, background, or skills.

John Maxwell warns against "trying to transplant a tomato plant into concrete. Even if you could get it to go into the ground, you know it isn't going to survive anyway."[81] Bill Hull said, "Call people who have prepared hearts. Often leaders spend more time trying to motivate people who aren't interested than they spend with those who are already interested. But bestowing responsibility on the unfaithful, the disinterested, and the carnal is the zenith of folly. Be on the lookout for the hungry hearts—those who are chomping at the bit to be established in the word of God, praying, fellowship, and witnessing."[82]

Your prospective disciples should be "fast, enthusiastic learners, displaying a capacity to absorb your advice, analyze it, and take it to heart."[83] They should be open to growth and change—not the type that spends their time in defensive mode. Look for vibrant, eager minds ready to catch God's fire and passion in you.

Establish LIFE Foundations at the Beginning

In our on-going ministry, we still begin with the five basic levels of discipleship mobilization considered in this book—confidence, consistency, stability, Christlikeness, and evangelism—before we go on to discipleship preparedness.[84] Our original ministry and various partners in East Africa, the Philippines, Germany, the USA, Southern Africa, and India have made good use of those tools. We have learned from our own thirty-year efforts, however, that when LIFE-inspired changes are lacking in any implementation of these basic levels, fruitful mobilization will not transpire.

Worldly confidence never leads to heavenly fruit. Life-centered patterns of consistency (or inconsistency) can never result in the fruitfulness God seeks in the lives of disciples. When LIFE is absent from confidence and consistency, its presence for stability through suffering will only be in matters of life-centered miracles of the body, not the soul. At the same time, there is no way to experience Christlikeness except by the presence of LIFE within. Discipleship mobilization of God's making is never accomplished by the mere imitation of Christ and the repetition of religious practices. Finally, evangelism without LIFE may result in converts, church members, and religious associations, but the result will be LIFE-less *evangelism* from them all.

> **33.** The entire book is summarized in simple fashion in the above paragraphs by looking at five basic levels of discipleship mobilization – confidence, consistency, stability, Christ-likeness, and evangelism. Which one, if any, of these summary statements has greatest impact on you? Copy to your journal and explain.

LIFE's presence in the initial stages of discipleship mobilization will feed the fruitful multiplication that is possible. We need to invite people to the dream walk, not just a walk, and to the dream-talk, not just a talk. A few books and tools will never be enough; only full-orbed LIFE-in-life living is the aim. Jesus had such an approach, and he wanted his disciples to first walk the dream with him before sending them out to help others walk the dream. The sacred dimension of discipleship was necessary to their lives because Jesus made disciples in that dimension. John learned to do so after a weak start. We can also come to that sacred dimension.

NOW, DISCIPLE SOMEONE

Yes, you can do it. That is the intent of this book. I urge you to use this tool or find another that will achieve the purpose.

- Begin by thinking of one person—a man for a man, a woman for a woman. Pray about that person. Seek God's guidance.
- Show them this book and your journal, and share your experience of reading and journaling.
- If you first read *God's Dream*, share the results of that reading for you, recommend it to the person, and tell them how they can purchase or order it.
- They may want to read the previous book first. It establishes the foundation for this series on *God's Dream*.
- Keep in touch with this person and ensure that he or she keeps you informed of their progress. You may decide to meet together and, among other things, talk about the book's content.
- At an appropriate time, ask if they would like to have a copy of *Dream-walking* and the *Dream-walking Journal*. If so, tell them how to purchase or order them. Explain the paper and electronic versions of the journal. Even some of the new-hand held gadgets can be used.
- When this person has his or her own copies, see if they can schedule weekly meetings with you over the next two to three months to discuss the book chapter-by-chapter. If you have agreed to journal, share what you have each written in your journals.
- Your meetings can be planned as each of you agree and can contain elements like fellowship, prayer, discussion of issues raised, a memory verse shared, and so on.
- Encourage the person, allowing for interruptions and changes of plans. Make use of today's mobile technology to stay in touch and make adjustments.
- If the person goes through the entire experience with you, they will arrive at this same page in their own book and, at that time, you can encourage them to find another person to disciple.
- In your own journal, keep track of the names of people you have discipled and those they have discipled. Try to go on to four generations, if not more. You will be humbled as you watch God at work.

- When you have a good group of people dream-walking with Jesus, plan other activities together as time and circumstances allow.[85]
- For some who want to be involved further, opportunities exist to make use of the Web version of these books to mentor some people in that way.
- For still others, the author of these books has established further online studies with a Christian university, giving you an opportunity to earn a diploma in discipleship mobilization and mentoring.[86] Go to www.Godsdreamrising.org for information.

I hope what was once for you just a walk with Jesus has become a dream-walk with him. I trust you have learned from John's experience, the experiences of others, and perhaps even my own. I pray that you now want to work with God to build confidence, consistency, stability, Christlikeness, evangelism, and discipleship into the life of others. Such efforts will be fruitful only with the sacred dimension of discipleship— —God's own LIFE in your life.

ENDNOTES

1. Larry L. Niemeyer, *God's Dream: A Refreshing Look at the Gospel* (Enumclaw, Washington: Wine Press Publishing, 2011).

2. Throughout *God's Dream* and this book, too, LIFE or LIFE always refers to God's divine life. Here, you will see the words innumerable times. Get used to it. Don't tire of it. I'm making a point. For too long, authors have referred to God's life with no distinction between it and our life. The distinction clarifies both the gospel and discipleship. It also clarifies God's relationship to us.

3. I refer to the tools we developed that eventually became packaged as *Foundations for Discipleship Mobilization* and *Fruitfulness in Discipleship Mobilization*, together with three supportive tools called *A Disciple-maker's Guide, Building Discipleship Foundations,* and *Bearing Discipleship Fruitfulness* (Nairobi, Kenya: Harvest Heralds, 2007).

4. Larry L. Niemeyer, *Discipling: A Kingdom Necessity in the African City* (Nairobi, Kenya: Harvest Heralds, 1999).

5. Donald C. Posterski, *Reinventing Evangelism* (Downer's Grove, Illinois: InterVarsity, 1989), 144-146.

6. Os Guinness, *Fit Bodies, Fat Minds* (Grand Rapids: Baker, 1994).

7. Larry L. Niemeyer, *Discipling: A Kingdom Priority* (Nairobi, Kenya: Harvest Heralds, 1996).

8. James Philip, "The Person of Christ" in *Bible Characters and Doctrines* (London: Scripture Union, 1973), 74-75.

9. W. Ian Thomas, *The Saving Life of Christ* (Grand Rapids, Michigan: Zondervan, 1961), 79-80.

10. Dallas Willard, *The Great Omission, Reclaiming Jesus' Essential Teachings on Discipleship* (San Francisco: HarperSanFrancisco, 2006), 17.

11. Eugene H. Peterson, *Tell it Slant: a conversation on the language of Jesus in his stories and prayers* (Grand Rapids, Michigan: Wm. B. Eerdmans, 2008), 161.

12. David C. Needham, *Birthright* (Portland, Oregon: Multnomah, 1979), 22.

13. E. Stanley Jones, *Christian Maturity* (New York: Abingdon-Cokesbury Press, 1952), 55.

14. A story told by Leonard Ravenhill according to John Maxwell, *Be All You Can Be: A Challenge to Stretch Your God-given Potential* (Colorado Springs, Colorado: Cook Communications Ministries, 2004 [1987], 37.

15. I like Eugene Peterson's explanation: "The phrase 'breathed on them' is the identical phrase (in Greek, *enephusêsen*) used in Genesis 2 when the Lord God breathed life into Adam, who at once became a 'living soul.' The Genesis 'in the beginning' that opens John's Gospel is now complemented by the Genesis 'breathed into his nostrils the breath of life' (Gen. 2:7) as Jesus breathes his life-creating Spirit into his disciples. The same Spirit that moved over the chaos and became articulate in the eight 'God said…' commands that created the heavens and the earth, now moves in the disciples so that they can continue the creation work of the 'firstborn of creation.'" Eugene Peterson, *Christ Plays in Ten Thousand Places* (Grand Rapids, Michigan: William B. Eerdman's, 2005), 106-107.

16. Selwyn Hughes, *Every Day with Jesus: Emblems of the Spirit* (Surrey, England: Crusade for World Revival, May/June 2007).

17. John Maxwell, *Failing Forward: Turning Mistakes into Stepping Stones for Success* (Nashville, Tennessee: Thomas Nelson, 2000), 40.

18. I have discussed these phenomena in *Discipling: A Kingdom Necessity in the African City* (Nairobi, Kenya: Harvest Heralds, 1999). The following notes, as well as others in subsequent chapters, are adapted from that book.

19. Kenneth J. Gergen, *The Saturated Self: Dilemmas of Identity in Contemporary Life* (New York: Basic, 1991), 18.

20. Adapted from Max DePree, *Leading without Power* (Holland, Michigan: Shepherd Foundation, 1997), 138.

21. The Watchman, *The Cutting Edge* (Nairobi, Kenya: *Daily Nation*, September 6, 1997), 7.

22. Greg Ogden, *Transforming Discipleship: Making Disciples a Few at a Time* (Downers Grove, Illinois: InterVarsity, 2003), 157.

23. Quoted by Tim Hansel, *Holy Sweat: The remarkable things ordinary people can do when they let God use them* (Dallas, Texas: Word, 1987), 85.

24. Vernon Grounds quoted in Tim Elmore, *Mentoring: How to Invest Your Life in Others* (Atlanta, Georgia: Equip, 2003), 75.

25. I again refer to my earlier book, *Discipling: a Kingdom Necessity in the African City* (Nairobi, Kenya: Harvest Heralds, 1996), 89-94.

26. Os Guinness, *Fit Bodies, Fat Minds* (Grand Rapids: Baker, 1994), 91.

27. Os Guinness, *Fit Bodies, Fat Minds*, 91.

28. Os Guinness, *Fit Bodies, Fat Minds*, 92.

29. George Barna, *Virtual America* (Ventura, California: Regal, 1994), 77.

30. Ibid.

31. Os Guinness, *Fit Bodies, Fat Minds* (Grand Rapids: Baker, 1994), 93.

32. Philip Yancey, *Reaching for the Invisible God* (Grand Rapids, Michigan: Zondervan, 2000), 169.

33. See Mark 8:35, John 16:33, and 2 Timothy 1:8, 3:12-13.

34. These quotations, in the order of their authorship, are found in Steve Miller, *C. H. Spurgeon on Spiritual Leadership* (Chicago:

Moody, 2003), 123; Gene Warr, "*What to Do when the Roof Falls In*," (Norman, Oklahoma: Discipleship Tape Library); Steve Miller, *C. H. Spurgeon on Spiritual Leadership*, 125; Calvin Miller quoted by Alan E. Nelson, *Broken in the Right Place: How God Tames the Soul* (Nashville, Thomas Nelson, 1994), 11; and Selwyn Hughes, *Every Day with Jesus: A Fresh Look at the Church* (Surrey, England, Crusade for World Revival, 2006), July 16.

35. See, for instance, the following: David Swartz, *Dancing with Broken Bones* (Colorado Springs, Colorado: NavPress, 1987); Alan E. Nelson, *Broken in the Right Place: How God Tames the Soul* (Nashville, Tennessee: Thomas Nelson, 1994); Kay Arthur, *Lord, Heal My Hurts* (Portland, Oregon: Multnomah, 1988); *Lord, Where Are You When Bad Things Happen?* (Sisters, Oregon: Questar Publishers, 1992); and *God, Are You There?* (Eugene, Oregon, Harvest House, 1994); Mark R. McMinn, *Making the Best of Stress* (Downer's Grove, Illinois: InterVarsity, 1996); Philip Yancey, *Where Is God When It Hurts?* (Grand Rapids, Michigan: Zondervan, 1977); R. C. Sproul, *Surprised by Suffering* (Wheaton, Illinois: Tyndale, 1988).

36. John Piper, *The Roots of Endurance: Invincible Perseverance in the Lives of John Newton, Charles Simeon, and William Wilberforce* (Wheaton, Illinois: Crossway, 2002).

37. In Alan E. Nelson, *Broken in the Right Place: How God Tames the Soul* (Nashville, Tennessee: Thomas Nelson, 1994), 67-68.

38. A reference to a bumper sticker in Barbara Johnson's book, *Stick a Geranium in Your Hat and Be Happy* (Dallas, Texas: Word, 1990), 106.

39. Mark 9:38 and Luke 9:54.

40. Adapted from Anthony DeStefano, *Ten Prayers God Always Says Yes To* (New York: Image/Doubleday, 2007), 59-60.

41. E. Stanley Jones, *The Christ of Every Road* (New York: Abingdon, 1930), 82-85.

42. Selwyn Hughes, *Every Day with Jesus: Hope Everlasting* (Surrey, England: Crusade for World Revival, 2006), 184.

43. Adapted from John Ortberg, *Most People Are Normal Until You Meet Them* (Grand Rapids, Michigan: Zondervan, 2003), 65-66.

44. Walt Emerson in Robert N. Bellah, Richard Madsen, William M. Sullivan, Ann Swidler, and Steven M. Tipton, *Habits of the Heart: Individualism and Commitment in American Life* (New York: Harper and Row, 1985), 63.

45. Ellen T. Charry, "The Crisis of Modernity and the Christian Self," *Theology, News and Notes* (Pasadena, California: Fuller Theological Seminary, October, 1996), 7-8.

46. David W. Henderson, *Culture Shift: Communicating God's Truth in Our Changing World* (Grand Rapids, Michigan: Baker, 1998), 103.

47. Robert H. Schuller, *Self-Esteem: The New Reformation* (Waco, Texas: Word, 1982), 158.

48. John F. Kavanaugh, *Still Following Christ in a Consumer Society* (Maryknoll, New York: Orbis, 1997), xxi, 11, 37.

49. James Strauss, "Trends and Triage in the Post Modern/Post Christian Culture" (Lincoln, Illinois: Lincoln Christian Seminary, 1993), 15.

50. Craig M. Gay, *The Way of the (Modern) World*, (Grand Rapids, Michigan: Wm. B. Ecrdmans, 1998), 209-210.

51. Os Guinness, *The Dust of Death* (Downers Grove, Illinois: InterVarsity, 1973), 136.

52. Greg Hawkins and Cally Parkinson, *Follow Me. What's Next for You?* (Barrington, Illinois: Willow Creek Association, 2008), 112-113.

53. Fllen T. Charry, "The Crisis of Modernity and the Christian Self" in *Theology, News and Notes* (Pasadena, California: Fuller Theological Seminary, October, 1996), 7-9.

54. Millard J. Erickson, *Postmodernizing the Faith: Evangelical Responses to the Challenge of Post-modernism* (Grand Rapids, Michigan: Baker, 1998), 98.

55. Jim Wallis, *God's Politics: Why the Right Gets It Wrong and the Left Doesn't Get It* (New York: HarperCollins, 2006), 31.

56. If so, the complexities increase as demonstrated in an explanation by Os Guinness: "Within America, the past generation has witnessed a titanic double shift: from the more traditional emphasis on individualism, with its accompanying concern

with majority rule, to the more recent emphasis on tribalism, with its accompanying concern with majority rights. These shifts have been followed in turn by lesser movement: from individual rights to group rights, from a concern for bread-and-butter policies to a concern for communal well-being, from an appeal to justice to an appeal to sensitivity, from legal redress to linguistic and psychic redress (or "emotional tort law"). Two of the more notable shifts have been a move from pluralism with a relativistic face to pluralism with a particularistic face, and from solutions based on respect for human dignity and civility to solutions based on rules and regulations." (Os Guinness, "More Victimized Than Thou," in Os Guinness and John Seel, Editors, *No God but God: Breaking with the Idols of Our Age* (Chicago, Illinois: Moody, 1992), 85.

57. John Mbiti, *African Philosophy and Religion* (London: Oxford, 1964), 60.

58. See, for example, Rom. 8:9-11; Gal. 4:19; 1 Cor. 1:30; 2 Cor. 4:6-12; 6:16; 13:3,5; Eph. 3:14-17; Col. 1:16, 3:11; and 2 Thess. 1:12.

59. Ronald T. Habermas, *The Complete Disciple: A Model for Cultivating God's Image in Us* (Colorado Springs, Colorado: NexGen/Cook Communications Ministries, 2003), 131.

60. Tim Hansel, *Holy Sweat: The remarkable things ordinary people can do when they let God use them* (Dallas, Texas: Word, 1987), 50.

61. W. Ian Thomas, *The Mystery of Godliness* (London: Pickering and Inglis, 1972), 25.

62. I am referring to the book called *Fruitfulness in Discipleship Mobilization* (Nairobi, Kenya: Harvest Heralds, 2009).

63. Author unknown.

64. Oswald Chambers, *Not Knowing Where: A Spiritual Journey through the Book of Genesis* (Grand Rapids, Michigan: Discovery House, 1989), 166.

65. Eugene H. Peterson, *Leap Over a Wall* (San Francisco: Harper Collins, 1997), 18.

66. Os Guinness and John Seel, Editors, *No God but God: Breaking with the Idols of Our Age* (Chicago, Illinois: Moody, 1993), 171.

67. Ibid, 171-173.

68. I have described these beginnings in two books: *Kingdom and Culture in Genesis*, and *Kingdom Faith: Breaking Through Religious Boundaries* (Nairobi, Kenya: Harvest Heralds, 2000).

69. J. D. Douglas, Editor, "Gnosticism," in *New Bible Dictionary*, Second Edition, (Leicester, England: Inter-Varsity, 1982), 425-426.

70. Lesslie Newbigin, *Foolishness to the Greeks: The Gospel and Western Culture* (Grand Rapids, Michigan: Wm. B. Eerdmans, 1987), 51.

71. Lesslie Newbigin, *Foolishness to the Greeks: The Gospel and Western Culture*, 51-55. (I agree with Newbigin except for his unfortunate reference to "true religion," which I believe is a poor reference to Christian faith.)

72. Raymond Brown, *Be My Disciple: Following Jesus in a Secular World* (London: Marshall Pickering, 1992), 9. (See John 1:29-37, 1:40-41, 1:43-46, 4:28-42, 9:1-34, 12:9-19, 20:31.)

73. An observation attributed to Bill Bright, (San Bernardino, California: Campus Crusade for Christ).

74. Ray Comfort, *The Way of the Master* (Orlando, Florida: Bridge-Logos, 2006), 256.

75. This contrast has been absent from English explanations, too, and attention has been given instead to "the person of God" (which translates very badly into many languages), God's "nature," and the "character of God," which is also weak.

76. Steven Barabas, "Gospel of John," *The New International Dictionary of the Bible* (Grand Rapids, Michigan: Zondervan, 1987), 533-536.

77. James Orr, General Editor, "Polycarp," and "Ireneaus," *International Standard Bible Encyclopedia*, Database, 2003 WORD search Corp.

78. Eugene H. Peterson, *Tell it Slant: a conversation on the language of Jesus in his stories and prayers* (Grand Rapids, Michigan: Wm. B. Eerdmans, 2008), 222-223.

79. Gene Warr, *You Can Make Disciples* (Waco, Texas: Word, 1978), 71.

80. Jim Collins, *Good to Great* (New York: HarperBusiness, 2001), 64.

81. John Maxwell, *The 360⁰ Leader: Developing Your Influence from Anywhere in the Organization* (Nashville, Tennessee: Thomas Nelson, 2005), 152.

82. Bill Hull, *Jesus Christ, Disciple-Maker* (Colorado Springs, Colorado: NavPress, 1984), 125.

83. Scott Snair, *Motivational Leadership: Surefire Strategies for Encouraging Cooperation* (New York: Alpha, 2007), 207.

84. These tools are available from Harvest Heralds, (email: larry@harvestheralds.org or USAharvest21@gmail.com. In East Africa, they are licensed to Harvest Impact Ministries (email: harvestimpact@gmail.com). Respective websites are www.harvest21.org and www.harvestimpacteafrica.org

85. The author's thirty-year involvement in this kind of ministry has resulted in many extra tools, books, and resources. Seminar materials are available for new disciplers and workshops materials are available for discipleship team leaders. Tools are also available for taking God's dream into communities and regions, combining the Great Commission of Matthew 28 with the Great Commandment of Matthew 22.

86. Entire diploma courses are available for discipleship mobilization with the distinguishing feature of having a LIFE-in-life unified curriculum. These courses are offered by the Harvest Institute of Harvest Heralds, Inc. (www.harvestheralds.org), and are offered in collaboration with Hope International University, Fullerton, California.

FOR MORE INFORMATION
Buy the first book in this series:
God's Dream: A Refreshing Look at the Gospel

Coming soon:
God's Dream-center: A Refreshing Look at the Church

Contact Larry L. Niemeyer
www.harvestheralds.org
http://larryniemeyer.authorweblog.com
larry@harvestheralds.org

WinePressPublishing
Great Books, Defined.

To order additional copies of this book call:
1-877-421-READ (7323)
or please visit our website at
www.WinePressbooks.com

If you enjoyed this quality custom-published book,
drop by our website for more books and information.

www.winepresspublishing.com
"Your partner in custom publishing."